How I Sell
$12,000,000 of Life Insurance
Year After Year

How I Sell $12,000,000 of Life Insurance Year After Year

By Karl Bach

His motto:
I don't sell insurance;
I help you buy it.

PACIFIC BOOKS, *Publishers*
Palo Alto, California

First printing May 1960
Second printing September 1960

To my adopted country, America,
that favored me with its benevolence;
and to the teeming numbers of its people
who accept life insurance as a noble idea.

A Profile
Karl Bach and Personal Selling

Nearly all selling is personal selling. Whether the product to be sold is a television set or a suspension bridge, the making or losing of the sale almost always comes right down to what one person can do to persuade one other person to buy. Advertising and other sales tools do their part and are of considerable value. After all the other moves have been made, the work of a salesman who talks with a buyer is the payoff.

Karl Bach is one of the great masters of personal selling. He makes a top-bracket income at it.

He makes much of his money by selling to "the man on the street"—the kind of customer the least-trained salesman can meet and sell. He makes more by selling to the more difficult customer, the kind that needs a highly trained and skilled salesman. And the "cream" of his income comes from selling to the most difficult customers, the ones for whom the sale demands expert technical planning to fit the merchandise to the particular problems of the customer.

Karl Bach has then something valuable to say to every kind

of salesman, as well as on every level of problem in the area of personal selling.

Every day, he faces that most personal of selling problems, the selling of insurance. He sells everything from the simplest policies to the complex plans involved in the technical intricacies of tax law, family finance, business finance, and estate planning.

Many of his "what to do and how to sell" illustrations will be expressed in terms of insurance selling problems. But all of them will be made clear so that they will be applicable to the personal selling of *all* kinds of products.

This is, then, a book for every salesman who sells anything whatever in personal, face-to-face interviews.

Karl Bach, Master Salesman

This book is neither a biography nor an autobiography of Karl Bach. It is a book for the salesman who wants to make more money at his work. But a word about the man will forward the purposes of the book.

Karl Bach was born in a small village in Germany. At the age of four, he suffered a polio attack which left its mark upon him,—but not enough of an injury to prevent him from driving his car, walking well, playing a fast game of table tennis, and even a bit of soccer.

He likes to talk about how lucky he always has been. And there is his first great lesson to the personal salesman: *"Always believe that your luck is helping you to win, even when all the apparent evidence seems to be against it."*

His parents ran a meat market. Each morning before school, Karl had to make the rounds of the neighborhood and get the meat orders for the day. He was shy, but like any small child, he assumed the people would treat him courteously and place their orders. And there is his second lesson to personal sales-men. *"I was lucky enough to develop early in life the attitude of always expecting to close business."*

His neighborhood was somewhat rough. He had competi-tors, other kids who were enduring the "hardships" of having to get out and sell before they could go to school. As a slightly lame little boy, he was a target for bullies. And he learned the third "lucky" lesson. *"A salesman who does not expect to have to fight once in a while should find some other way to earn his living."*

After school, he had to go to the meat market and help pre-pare the orders he had taken in the morning. Then he had to deliver them. From this experience developed another of his philosophies in selling. *"You have to take personal responsi-bility for making sure that the merchandise is what the cus-tomer expects it to be. You can't blame your boss and apolo-gize to your customers if you want to build a clientele."*

When Hitler began to show that he could do what he threatened to do, the Bach family came to the United States. The experience was severe. The Bachs had to walk away from all that they had built up in their business. But as Karl looks at it, "I was lucky enough to be in a family that realized that *when the time comes to move, make your move, and don't worry about what you might lose by it."* That, of course, is a lesson that salesmen should learn early in their careers.

Karl Bach landed in New York with about ten dollars in his pocket, no job, and little knowledge of the English language. He was twenty years old. The great depression was in full swing. But he was probably the only man in the city who did not believe that a depression existed. Before he had even so much as gotten off the boat, he had seen those endless parades of great big, beautiful automobiles all over the streets. All he could see was prosperity. His lesson to salesmen: *"Never think gloom and never talk gloom. If you look for good you will find it."*

One casual glance showed him that none of the streets was paved with gold. He had heard about the prestige "glamor" jobs that could be had in New York. But what he wanted was cash, cash right now, so he could eat and have a place to sleep. To salesmen he says, *"Go for the cash. If you earn prestige it will come to you. But cash is what counts."*

He quickly found his way to a meat packing house where his training as a butcher could earn him his living. "Salesmen have instincts. *If you are willing to sell what you have for sale, then you can smell your way to the man who needs to buy it."*

The Master Key to His Working Methods

A line of men seeking jobs had formed at the door of that meat packing establishment. Briefly, Karl Bach stood at the end of that line. Soon, however, he realized this would give him little chance for a job.

If he had known anything about baseball, he might have said that in that line he had three strikes on him before he ever picked up the bat. Count them. He had a physical defect —a slight limp. He had a language problem, for he knew only a little English. And further, he had no record of employment in the United States and could offer no local reference about his previous experience.

Karl Bach got out of that line. He walked around to the back door of the plant. There, he found a man who could talk with him. In a few minutes the man took him through the back door and introduced him to a foreman. The foreman hired him. *"If you want to sell, then give yourself a chance."* You will find that master-key working method, in one form and another, all through the pages of this book.

He started to work at once. *"The time to start working is right now."*

By getting out of that line and going to the back door he had given himself a chance. *"Luck is on the side of the man who gives it a solid chance to work for him."* His job was on a gallery. He was beside a window through which he could see the street in front of the plant. He devoted about half of a second to looking out at that line of men. The line did not seem to move a step. Then he turned to his work. *"Give yourself to your work, and your work will give you your money."*

He worked for thirty cents an hour, often sixty hours a week. He was just about the only man in the plant who did not feel abused, degraded and exploited. Translated into German marks his earnings seemed princely. He was used to even longer hours and harder work. *"Stick to your selling. Promotion to a job with a title is bunk.* Unless you become President of the United States you can't get promoted to *any* job that some other man will not look upon with contempt."

Sixty hours of work, night school, studying to become a citizen, week after week, and yet he managed to save money.

"Don't Come! There Are No Opportunities Here!"

Most of the Bach family had gone on to California. Karl decided to join them. He queried an uncle in Stockton, California. The uncle wrote back, "Stay where you are. There are no opportunities in California."

Karl got on a bus which was headed west. He says to good personal salesmen, *"If you are in the United States, then opportunity is wherever you happen to be."*

In magazine-article descriptions of his life, humorous copy has been made of the fact that in California the butchers' union would not let him work as a meat cutter, and so he had to quit his trade and become a highly paid personal salesman. But the fact is, he was quite ready to turn to the much greater opportunities of salesmanship. *"Don't hang around the small change any longer than it takes you to get ready to reach for the bigger money."*

Once more he gave himself a chance.

The one "help wanted" advertisement that seemed to promise to get him into selling in the least time and with the least bother was that of the Fuller Brush Man. By studying his "how to sell" manuals, by working hard, and by always giving himself a chance, he got up to the top ranks of the Fuller men. *"Never stop learning your trade. The salesman who knows too little sells too little."*

What He Did, You Can Do

He turned to insurance selling because it offered more dollars of commission per sale. He was young. He is only forty-two right now.

Karl Bach won't tell how much money he makes a year. But he was the first Penn Mutual Life Insurance Company agent to sell more than $3,000,000 worth in one year. Then he became the first to sell more than $5,000,000 worth in one year. Only one general agency in ten (a general agency is a branch office which employs groups of "agents" or salesmen) sells as much as Karl does as an individual.

His word to salesmen is *"What any other salesman can do, I can do. And what I can do, any other salesman can do."*

He Really Follows His Own Principles—Karl Bach Today

Everyone who meets Karl Bach and hears him talk about his methods says, "This can't be all. There must be some trick he is holding back."

Meet him. A quiet, well-mannered, average-sized man comes forward to greet you. There are no loud or flashy clothes, no trick eyeglasses with which to make gestures, no unusual haircut, no attention-catching special mannerisms, nothing that says or symbolizes, "I am a great salesman."

His home is spacious, gracious and beautiful, but completely free of ostentation. Wide lawns, ample play space for his six healthy children, a large-roomed and well-planned ranch-type house, tastefully furnished, but no clutter. Big trees in the garden, beautiful flower beds, swimming pool, all spell casual living at its best, but absolutely nothing in the whole setting says "I am a master salesman and here I entertain important customers." Meryl, his wife, is beautiful, gracious, charming and intelligent. But she too is quiet. She fits those surroundings.

It all seems too quiet, so "un-salesmanlike."

From your first minute with Karl Bach you feel that he is finding out what you want and is helping you to get it. You feel confident, energized. And even if you are with him for several weeks, the feeling does not die down.

Free energy salesmanship is all there is to the success of Karl Bach. He has no trick methods. He has only what he is going to tell *you* to use. It made a fortune for him. It will make one for you.

Edwin Laird Cady

January 14, 1960

. . . Contents

Part II

The Journeyman—Stage Two

Part III

The Advanced Salesman—Stage Three
Taking the Third Stride

Part IV

Estate Planning—Helping People to Die "For All They Are Worth" Taxwise

Part V

A Panoramic Survey

PART I
The Apprentice
Stage One

*The First Stride Toward
a Salesman's Success*

1

Free Energy Salesman-
ship—What It Is

When you fill a teakettle full of cold water and put it on
a hot stove there are two ways to describe what happens.

You can say that the stove forces heat into the water. Or
you can say that the water draws or pulls heat from the stove.

For purposes of talking about salesmanship I like the idea
that the water draws the heat out of the stove.

The salesman is the stove. The teakettle is the prospect.
The cup of tea that you make with the boiling water is the
profit on the sale.

Let's say that it is a coal stove that we have. The energy
to heat the water has been in the coal millions of years,
but it hasn't been heating anything. You have to set fire to
the coal. The fire liberates that energy, sets it free so it can
go to work. Isn't it thus with fissionable material?

That's the simple principle of free energy salesmanship.
You have a hot salesman, a cold prospect, and a sale to be
made for profit.

When the sale is made the prospect becomes a customer.

3

But if the customer doesn't return for another cup of tea, then you have not made a client out of that customer.

Sales make money. But you have to have clients if you want to get rich. The gravy is in the successive or "repeat" sales.

You can also put a hot teakettle on a cold stove. But if you do, then the water will get cooler without the stove getting much warmer. And that is no way to make hot tea. But I think you will agree that when the kettle touches the stove, and the stove is already hot and ready for its job, the water begins to draw upon that heat.

The salesman has to have free energy. He has to cause the prospect to draw that energy from him. You will see that I am sold on that idea expressed in my slogan, *"I don't sell insurance, I help you buy it."* (More about this later.)

The Prospect Must Keep on Drawing Energy

My concept of free energy applies to a prospect who realizes a need, and then keeps on drawing upon the salesman for more and more information, more and more of the energy of action, until the need is fully satisfied.

Unless the prospect is first to realize his need, the salesman must make him feel and recognize it. Every prospect has built-in resistance, which requires the use of his energy. But this energy can be diverted into other channels and help make the sale.

2

For Hard-Sell or Soft-Sell, Use Energy-Sell

I understand it to be "hard-sell" when you overwhelm your prospect with the sheer force of your arguments, the "special features," and "buy right now or else you will lose something" techniques. I don't do much of that. When in rare instances, however, I have to do it, the free energy idea works well.

Here is an example:

Three partners were thinking about "taking out" business life insurance to cover each other's interest. They were hesitating, considering one idea and another, talking to me and to my competitors. I couldn't get the partners to close, but I could keep them drawing upon me for facts pertaining to various insurance plans and for miscellaneous information. Also, in our talks I got a fairly clear picture of what was most suitable for their needs.

In every business, there is some kind of "right now" period in which the prospect must either buy or lose something. One of these "right now's" is the "age-change date," the day mid-

5

way between the prospect's last and next birthdays. For insurance purposes, he becomes one year older on that date; consequently, the rate increases.

I kept the partners drawing upon me by keeping the current flowing, until the age-change date of the senior partner was at hand. Then I requested a conference. At this meeting, the partners produced a heap of written proposals by my competitors, but I had the actual policies to put before them. The policies incorporated all the features necessary to meet the requirements of these men. I said, "Here are your policies. You will take them right now, or you will never again get them at this all-time low rate."

All three partners closed with me then and there. But I never would have made that close, if I had not kept those partners drawing upon me for energy until the time for the hard-sell was ripe.

The dual advantage of lower rates and having the actual policies at hand was the source of the free energy and the successful outcome—the sale.

"Soft-sell," I understand, is when you give your prospect a little information, and perhaps let him try the merchandise at his leisure, and then you leave him largely alone to make his decision.

I don't do much of that. But, on the occasions when I must do so, I use the aid of free energy. This is an illustration:

A referred prospect definitely needed life insurance, but I could not stir him into taking any action. So I kept the current turned on, with a bit of soft-selling. I said, "Don't be in a hurry before you get all the facts." I gave him no literature to sit on. Instead I just kept whetting his curiosity by keeping open the door for further discussion.

He invited me to his home. He handed me a batch of lithographed proposals which soft-selling competitors had left with him. He said, "Put your proposition in figures, leave it with me, and I'll make a comparison with the other proposals I have."

I replied, "Where is your wastebasket?" With a firm but undramatic manner, I placed the other proposals in it. "Until you have had your physical examination so that the company can determine how good a risk you are, these proposals are meaningless and belong with the rest of the scrap paper," I remarked.

"May I use your phone?" I asked.

Using his telephone, I made an immediate appointment to have him examined. He kept the appointment. He had been in close touch with a source of the energy of action. He was beginning to draw strong energy from it.

We had to wait several days for the medical report of his examination. While we waited, we had more interviews. His questions kept on drawing from me further information related to his situation.

I closed him. There was no trick to the closing. He gave me his check. Thus by simply signing his name he had added many estate dollars for his family—at once.

In turn, I experienced a real thrill out of this sale, as always, by helping him make a sound decision for the benefit of his family.

When a softly-sold man gets free energy of action from a salesman, he sticks to that salesman. He likes to be energized. All of us do. You do. So do I.

That is what I mean by free energy salesmanship.

The prospect has a need. He draws energy from the salesmanship of the salesman, and thus he gets the energy for the buying action that will fill his need. All the energy comes from the salesman. The drawing upon the energy is done by the prospect.

Any salesman can raise his production and his income with that method. All he needs is to have a source of good merchandise, and a way of getting in touch with good prospects.

A live wire is dead until it is connected at both ends.

Free energy must be harnessed and channeled into the proper circuit. The switch the salesman uses to accomplish this is his resourcefulness. A mild shock in the form of a properly timed single action on the part of the salesman, can achieve a combination of results.

It has been said that Edison invented the phonograph to keep us awake, so we would stay up all night using his electric lights.

3

What to Do First
Every Morning

Start every business day by selling yourself *on* yourself.

You have to set fire to that coal, or put a spark to that gasoline, before there can be any free energy to put action into the prospect. You have to set yourself on fire. Until you are sold on yourself for the day, you will stand very little chance of selling anybody anything. But when you are sold on yourself, then you can sell anybody anything which you understand well enough to sell and which anybody ought to buy.

I recommend silent prayers, but that is as far as I want to go into the subject of religion. Face the Supreme Being with strong faith that you are doing a job that needs to be done, and you'll be a strong man for the day.

At meetings I have seen sales managers gather their men into groups and have them sing, whistle, clap their hands and stamp their feet to work up enthusiasm. It works! But I am not much of a "whoop" and "yell" guy myself. Rather, I want to sell you on creating within yourself a strong and abiding confidence in the value of the job you are doing and in your ability to do that job well.

9

I read an article which told how a certain author starts his day by writing himself a letter telling himself what a good writer he is. You don't have to go that far. But his procedure is along the lines I feel you can use to advantage.

Vary what you tell yourself in accordance with the line you sell and the conditions under which you sell it. But start every business day by making a sales talk to yourself. Here is an example of such a self-selling soliloquy which will help every salesman turn on his free energy.

Why I Am Glad I Am a Salesman—Why Every Day Is Thanksgiving Day to Me

"Today I shall sell merchandise that will benefit the buyers more than the selling of it will benefit me. I can face all men with the happy thought that I am giving more than I expect to get back.

"Because I shall work, others will have jobs. If salesmen were not selling, then no wheel would turn in any factory, nor on any highway or railroad. I am a salesman. I create jobs, my own and those of other men.

"For all of this I shall be well paid.

"I will be talking to a number of men. Nearly all men are friendly, kind and polite. Talking is fun, as all men know. I shall have that fun. It is nice to get paid for having fun.

"My work is personal. It is man to man. No machine can threaten my job. No machine can limit my pay nor force me to learn a new skill in order to make a good livelihood. I am immune in my vocation to the threat of automation that frightens so many highly skilled men.

"There is no wage ceiling in my work, either. The more skill I can develop in selling, the more pay I can receive. There is always a limited number of highly skilled salesmen. There always will be. Some of the highest paid jobs in the world are essentially selling jobs, though frequently designated by other titles. There always will be better pay for me as I develop better skills of salesmanship. The better I learn to sell and the more effective I become in my work, the higher I can reach.

"Whether I am paid on the basis of salary, commission, or any other arrangement, I come as close to being an independent business man as anyone can in our time. With little exception, there is no 'boss' to look over my shoulder and dictate to me as I do my work. For the most part, I am on my own. Like any other worker, I produce 'or else.' But the need for my services is so great, that if I show a reasonable degree of diligence and potential, there never need be any 'or else' to worry about.

"Yes, I am an independent business man. But I am free of the weighty problems that confound the self-employed business man.

"I have no large investment of capital, and no financier controls my business.

"I am not burdened with inventory.

"I have no labor problems. Labor-union negotiations on manpower or wage demands never confront me in my operation. I am not required to spend much time at conferences except in selling to prospects.

"Every year the seed is planted for my next year's harvest. My job and my income will continue.

"I have heard about men having to pass civil service examinations before qualifying for jobs at raking leaves in the park. In my work, performance in actual selling is the determining test. If I can sell, then I can have the job and the money.

"No requirement for formalized training can hold me

down. In the field of selling, there are highly educated men as well as those with only a minimum formal education. The successful salesmen come from both ranks, as do the failures.

"I cannot depreciate the value of formal education when it is fully realized; however, we all know many college graduates who reflect very little 'higher learning.' By the same token, we have also seen many self-educated men who have risen far beyond them. It is, therefore, *you*—the individual—who ultimately determines your success or failure in selling.

"Each year I become a year older. So does everyone else. But there lies the difference.

"The other fellow is working toward enforced retirement. In one job after another, I see men summarily eliminated by a mandatory retirement ruling. That need never happen to me. True, I enjoy all the retirement as well as other fringe benefits that other men have. I can retire voluntarily, but supposing I choose to retire and don't enjoy it?

"There is always a place for good personal salesmanship. Men and women in their eighties are selling and making big money out of it. Possibly the money will have less meaning for me when I get older, but the satisfaction in knowing that I am doing a job that needs to be done will always be an important value to me. As long as I am capable of working, there will always be a job for me. No arbitrary retirement-age restrictions will handicap me.

"Yes, this morning I am glad that I am a salesman!

"I am doing a job of real value and dignity, a job to which men pay high honor.

"My job has a most promising 'right now' as well as a future.

"And now I am going to go out. I am going to have the pleasure of talking with people, the challenge of the contest, and the satisfaction of giving more than I receive—an important service.

"To me, selling is not an ordeal or a form of drudgery, but a genuine challenge and crusade. It is a way of transmitting knowledge to people, a way of offering valuable and sincere guidance to people."

Consider these thoughts of thanksgiving and give them real meaning by feeling them. When you are thoroughly convinced of the worth, the dignity, and the limitless future of effective salesmanship, your success will be inevitable.

4

Attitude Means More Than Aptitude

In the earlier chapters, I advocated a positive *attitude* toward salesmanship and toward yourself as a salesman.

I have seen a number of so-called "natural-born salesmen." Some have risen to the top levels in the field of selling, but most of them stayed at the bottom. They strike out too often. "Flair" or a strong aptitude for selling won't get you into the big time unless you back it up with the right attitude.

There are vocational tests to measure your aptitude for selling. Of course, the clock can't be turned back for me to take such a test before starting my career. But I would be willing to bet my shirt that I would have flunked such a test by the biggest minus score of all time. No one ever yet has looked at me and said, "There goes a good example of the natural-born salesman."

Attitude toward my job has won for me.

It will win for you, too.

You Can't Conceal Your Attitude

Later in this book you will be told that every salesman must be an actor at times. But there is one way in which your acting ability will fail you.

No acting skill will conceal your attitude from your prospect. Every salesman unwittingly communicates with his prospect. It may be an unconscious process manifested by voice, gestures, facial expression, or just the general manner. I'm not sure how it functions, but I do know that the communication exists.

Your attitude may be deep within you, so deep that you are not even aware of it. I have lost more than one "dead cinch" sale, and upon a post-mortem analysis of the interview, I found that without realizing it, I had been harboring some bad feeling toward the prospect. My surface attitude had been perfect, but I could not stop my subconscious mind from meddling in the interview and getting into the act.

How to Acquire Successful Salesmanship Attitudes

First, maintain a good-will attitude toward all mankind. Any taint of prejudice will show up as lost sales. Many a proud and fervid member of an "anti" group would resign at once if he knew how many dollars his prejudices were costing him.

In this I am lucky. I have never heard my mother say or imply anything evil about any human being. She still lives an active life. From my infancy she has taught me to think well of all men. This is an attitude that you may have to acquire if you want the fastest and easiest road to the top rewards of salesmanship. An open mind toward people means an open door to their good will.

Always think of the prospect as a friend. And he is your friend. He deserves your friendship. Start to reciprocate for his friendship even before he shows you any. With that thought about him you are apt to establish a mutually profitable friendship on your first interview with any prospect. I take the attitude that if I can't regard the prospect as a friend, then I can't sell him. I give myself away to a prospect before I can hope to get anything from him. It is my idea of affection for people. I never *weigh* what I give *away*.

Always Expect to Sell—Always Consider Yourself as an "Engineer of Consent"

In this I have been lucky. As a young schoolboy in a small town in Germany I had to get up early and go out to get the neighborhood orders for my father's butcher shop. I accepted the "I expect to get orders when I ask for them" attitude as easily and naturally as a young child absorbs everything else.

If you don't expect to sell, then the prospect will detect this in you, and you probably will not sell. I have known great sales managers to require a salesman to spend his nights behind a retail counter until that "expect to sell" attitude got into him.

A lot of soul searching goes into teaching yourself to be a salesman. If you can analyze any interview and find that you went into it with "maybe I can sell him, but I don't expect to in this interview" on your mind, then do something to purge yourself of that feeling. It is cowardice. You are excusing yourself for losing before the fight has even begun.

Advance alibis are a luxury no salesman can afford. There are excuses for failure only when there are no opportunities for success.

On the wall of my office, framed and in prominent view at

all times, is this expression of a stouthearted boxing champion's attitude. To me its simple eloquence is inspiring.

COURAGE

Fight one more round. When your feet are so tired that you have to shuffle back to the center of the ring, fight one more round. When your arms are so tired that you can hardly lift your hands to come on guard, fight one more round. When your nose is bleeding and your eyes are black and you are so tired that you wish your opponent would crack you one on the jaw and put you to sleep, fight one more round—remembering that the man who always fights one more round is never whipped.

JAMES J. CORBETT

Always Expect to Find the Money—"Cherchez Le Dough"

In my family room at home is a $1,500 high-fidelity set. When I bought it, I was putting every cent I could raise into investments. A $150 television set was affording me plenty of relaxed entertainment. Yet, a salesman sold me on that hi-fi. And when he did, I somehow found the money for it.

Now that I have done *my* bit of confessing, you look into *your* life. You will find one item after another that you "couldn't afford." But when someone sold it to you, you found the money for it.

Always take the attitude that any man will, within reason, find the money for anything he really wants.

The same thing holds true when you are trying to sell a company that "can't find the money in its budget."

If your prospect can't find the money, then you have not done an effective selling job. You have offered the wrong merchandise, or you have handled him poorly.

To become clients, prospects must have money for your

merchandise. It's that simple! It is part of the salesman's job to explore for and locate the money.

It is your job to make him want your merchandise more than he wants his money. If you are acting in his behalf, then the task is not too difficult.

Always Be Sure That You Are the Energy Source

When a prospect convinces you that he can't afford to buy, then one of two things has happened. Either you have been wrong in considering him a prospect, or *he* has become the free energy source and *you* have become the energized subject.

It is one of the oldest axioms of salesmanship. "*Always* sell the prospect. *Never* let the prospect sell you."

Only last week, I concluded an interview fully convinced that the prospect did not have the money to buy the insurance I had offered him. He had *sold* me on the idea. But before I had driven my car half a mile from his house, I thought it over. I turned my car around and decided to return. He was surprised to see me.

"I became interested in seeing that new boat of yours that's eating up all of your cash in its monthly payments," I said. "Would you show it to me? I'll drive you out to the harbor and back."

He agreed. The boat really was a beautiful craft. "Do you have her fully insured against all hazards?" I asked.

"Of course," he said. "The finance company requires it, and I would want it that way for the protection of my family."

Then I said, "But there is one hazard you have left unprotected—your untimely death. Your family would lose the boat in that event. So you haven't really protected your family against all losses, certainly not the most serious one."

He got the point. He bought the life insurance to cover his family against all the things they might lose if he were to cease being around to pay for them. And he found the money to pay for it.

It Works While You Sleep

Here are some signs that indicate you are taking the *wrong* attitude and approach toward effective salesmanship.

—You worry about what a prospect might do while the sale hangs fire, and your anxiety undermines your positive attitude toward him.

—You divert yourself through any one of the "seven deadly sins," as in the Bible. Every salesman needs a side line, but this form of escape is not constructive, only destructive.

—You can't sleep without tranquilizers or sleeping pills.

Take the right attitude. You will have friends everywhere, even though you haven't met all of them yet. You will expect to sell. You will maintain control of your interviews. You will sell. You will enjoy your relaxations. And you will sleep soundly and restfully at night.

You will make money. As Mike Todd once said, "I've never been poor—only broke. Being poor is a frame of mind; being broke is a temporary condition."

5

Be Willing to Serve
Your Apprenticeship

I have had to go through three stages of salesmanship. I call them "apprentice," "journeyman" and "advanced." The apprentice is just learning how to use the tools of his trade. The journeyman is an experienced salesman, able to handle the sales that bring in a larger income. The advanced man is fit for the complex affairs that put him into the "big time" —the major leagues.

When I was an apprentice, I could not have sold the kinds of business I closed later as a journeyman. In my first month of selling insurance, all my cases were turned back by the medical examiners and I earned nothing. In my second month, I had much the same record, but I did manage to make six dollars. If I had had the training of a journeyman, I would have known how to be selective in my prospecting. The proof of this is that by the time my selling reached the journeyman stage I was making $20,000 a year out of free energy personal salesmanship.

Before getting into the ranks of the advanced men, I had to work hard at learning more of the selling craft.

This meant refueling, which involved putting the same facts together, but drawing fresh conclusions.

Since my market was people, I was compelled to do some market research to find what motivated them. Incidentally, this is still my constant study. When I found new uses for my product, which is life insurance, then I felt that I had arrived—at the *postgraduate milestone.* The studying of other men's methods has characterized my whole insurance career. I am still learning to sell. I am still fervently searching for something more in selling methods and experimenting with new ideas.

Memorize the Sales Talks During the Apprenticeship Stage

My introduction to the business of selling was as a Fuller Brush Man. As usual, I was fortunate. My good fortune was in the fact that I didn't think I knew how to sell. I was given three sales talks to learn. I memorized them as well as I could. Armed with these and a lot of hard work and training, I made enough money to get married. In fact, I developed my income to $10,000 a year by door-to-door selling of Fuller products.

A friend showed me that the commission per sale on life insurance was far more remunerative. So I proceeded to sell insurance in the evenings while continuing with my Fuller products by day until I was able to establish my insurance selling adequately. I have never believed that a man should gamble with his time. Keeping a firm grip on time is part of keeping the firm control necessary for free energy salesmanship.

In the life insurance business, too, there were sales talks to learn. And again I learned them. Call them "canned sales talks" if you will, but don't depreciate their worth. It is better to have a sales talk which has been devised by professionals and its effectiveness tried and tested than an original sales approach by an inexperienced amateur.

I am still an apprentice in that respect. Whenever I get a new type of insurance to sell, I obtain the standard sales talks on it, memorize and use them. Since my rote memory is not perfect, I probably never really use the same talk in the same way twice.

Standard sales talks produce results. Don't hesitate to use them. They have been developed after careful study and analysis and can be a real asset to you in selling. They constitute a ready source of free energy for every salesman.

Learn from All Sources

I try to interview all salesmen who call on me. They get a fair chance to sell me. But my greatest profit is in what they teach me. Day after day I learn from them.

One of them said, "This gift will intrigue the prospect"—a pause—"you agree, don't you?"

I used that two-second pause followed by "You agree, don't you?" in my next interview. It worked.

Direct-mail sales literature I take home to read. In that way, I save my business hours for selling. In the quiet of my den, I can appreciate and evaluate the headline salesmanship of direct mail, and emulate, in my own work, the ideas advanced, or the ideas it has stimulated.

A headline of one such direct-mail folder screamed at me, "In just fifteen minutes you can increase your peace of mind." That one also works well in my interviews, except that I revised it by adding, "It could be accomplished with a mere signature."

Books on salesmanship I take home for study. I read and digest them thoroughly. One such book told me to call upon druggists in their quiet period, just between the rush of the afternoon and the hurry of the evening hours. I have sold a lot of druggists that way during those hours.

If you have picked up this book, expecting that it will reveal the magical secrets or success formula of a man who knows everything, or that it is a grab bag bursting with pat ideas on salesmanship, then put it down. No man can hope to know all about the craft of salesmanship. I can only tell you what works well for me. Taking the attitude that I am still an apprentice keeps my ego from swelling.

Pride Can Make the Clock Hands Stand Still

Approach all new ideas with your eyes open and your mouth shut, not the reverse. Invest your time in listening to the idea, not to yourself. Pride of your own opinion tends to make you static. Static means you are standing still.

Some salesmen are too proud to read direct mail. When you say "that darned stuff comes in by the bushel," and you throw it into the wastebasket, then you begin to believe that the advertising your company sends out is "wastebasket stuff" also. With that, you fail to give full value to your company's advertising.

Direct-mail is created by some of the best brains in the sales business, and you have much to learn from it. I do. Take time for it, but not time that should be used to make appointments for sales interviews.

Call in the Experts—Don't Steal the Show

When a prospect asks you questions you are not equipped to answer, your best solution is to say, "I don't know, but I know someone who does."

You can bluff, of course, but bluff is poor fuel for the fires of free energy salesmanship. Even if it is necessary to share the credit or commission with the man you call in, half of something is better than all of nothing. And nothing is what bluffing is most likely to get you. As I have said, there is communication in an interview, other than the spoken word. The fact that you are bluffing will transmit itself.

An apprentice has to call in the expert far more often than does a journeyman. But not even the advanced man is beyond the need of expert advice. What I pay out annually to experts who help me would support a number of good salesmen. So, you see, I am still an apprentice in that regard also.

Learn how to use expert associates right now.

There are two important things to remember. The first is to call in the joint salesman or expert when things *begin* to go wrong, and not to wait until the whole house is burning down. The second is to know how to support him and build him up.

In this age of specialization, few of us, even the most skilled do-it-yourselfers, can do all the work singlehandedly. I feel it is my duty to entrust many of my clients' problems to someone who is more qualified than I. I feel it my obligation to my clients to see that they have the best possible advice and guidance.

Moreover, I get full credit for the *final* result, regardless of the modest part I have played in it.

You and the Expert

You will be told many times in this book that a salesman must be an actor. This is never more important than when you accompany either an expert or a fellow salesman to an interview.

You will see him try something on the prospect, and you will think, "That can't possibly succeed."

You will find that his "impossible" method does work.

When you think "impossible," don't let your face react "impossible." Look positive. Be *with* the man, but practice restraint. Don't "mug." Don't nod your head violently. Don't overact. If you do, the whole interview will look silly.

Place yourself properly, insofar as the conditions or the setting of the interview will permit.

If you sit beside the expert you accompany, then you will be directly under the observation of the prospect.

If you sit beside the prospect, but too far out of his line of vision, then he will feel as if he had one enemy in front and another behind him. Remember, there must be free energy in the interview. You are part of the energy supply upon which the prospect is drawing. You must not make him feel he is being heated from two directions at once.

The best arrangement is a right-angle triangle. Observe the direct line of vision between your expert and your prospect. Sit so that you face the prospect and you are at one side of your expert, and at about equal distance from the side of the expert as is the prospect.

Be out of the line of fire, but stay within the field of the interview. Obviously, you'll have to adjust your seating to the place and the furniture arrangement.

Be ready for carom shots.

Let's say that you are "Tom" and the expert you accompany is "Bill."

Don't be taken off guard if you hear Bill say, "Our proposition is the flywheel of every man's future"—laugh—"I say that for the sake of Tom here."

As a good salesman, Bill will use every tool he finds available. You are available. He has hit the prospect with a power statement. It might have hit too hard. He has softened it by pretending that it landed on you, the apprentice observer, and then bounced over and hit the prospect. He has made the prospect a teammate and ally in your training.

Supposing at that point your pride were to cause you to say, "I already knew that one." (Yes, those things do happen!) You can see how the interview could go down the drain.

How to Introduce the Expert

In the chapter on "What To Do First Every Morning" you were told to say to yourself, "I shall be well paid."

Leave that idea completely behind you when you go into the interview. Call it superstition if you will, but I have found it almost invariably fatal to think about my commission when I am either planning or making a sale. What I am giving you here reflects the *selling attitudes* that enabled me to sell $12,000,000 a year of insurance for the past several years; most of it to prospects that you or *any* reasonably good salesman can approach and sell.

Concentrate completely on how your prospect will benefit, and how you will enable him to enjoy those benefits. Then, you will sell.

With that one reservation—that the prospect's interests are paramount—you and the expert must agree in advance on how the interview is to be started. The start will depend on the situation you face at the time. The number of possible situations is limitless. Usually you will face one of the following three:

1. The expert is expected to take over completely, so you say to your prospect, "Mr. Smith, here is Bill Jones, the man who knows all that I don't know about what you need to know."

2. You repeat what you previously told the prospect about the importance of his affairs and why these deserve the best possible treatment. You say, "Mr. Smith, I feel that your affairs will be in the best shape only if the matter which I discussed with you before is handled correctly. I feel so strongly on this point that I have brought along Bill Jones who is highly trained and experienced in that subject." Then you proceed to build up Bill Jones and his qualifications in that area.

3. You have thought of some new sales arguments since the previous interview. You now play a carom shot. It hits Bill, the expert, and bounces off him, hitting the prospect. You say, "Mr. Smith I have told our expert, Bill Jones, something about your situation, but I don't think I've given him sufficient data. In any event, we should review the facts I have furnished him so he can evaluate them better. Will you help me with that please?"

Mr. Smith is not likely to refuse. I have never seen a prospect refuse to play his part in an act which is put on for the benefit of the guest, the expert.

You go completely through your previous presentation, bringing in new arguments if you have any, stressing the factors on which the prospect agreed in the previous interview, letting the prospect talk if he will.

Be prepared for surprises.

At this interview, the prospect may announce that he is no

longer disturbed by the particular problem that necessitated the assistance of your expert. Or, the prospect may now object to points on which he had hitherto agreed. He may even bring up new issues for discussion.

Here you have a very dramatic turning point—it can happen. I know, because it has actually occurred in my experience. My expert hadn't even gotten started. Your sale can be killed unless you close the instant the prospect is ready to close, even if this should occur before the social amenities have been completed.

That possibility is a severe test of your strategy as a salesman and also that of your expert. *You must close if the prospect is ready to close.* On this point, you and your expert must have a thorough understanding *before* meeting with your prospect and cooperate with each other fully. Regardless of how meticulously you both planned out the interview, if the prospect indicates he is ready to close, you and your expert must recognize this immediately and proceed to close then and there. This takes precedence over any presentation or material you have prepared to discuss. Pay your expert in full just as though he had completed his full service at the interview; however, should you require his assistance in handling certain details of the transaction, he is obliged to fulfill the full cycle of his service to you.

If that situation does not arise, then guide the interview to the subject on which Bill Jones is an expert. At that point, pass the ball to Bill, and be sure you get out of his way. Don't run interference for him.

The teamwork of the apprentice and the expert has accomplished thousands of "impossible" sales. It can close some for you also. And remember, someday you, too, will be an expert, extending assistance to other apprentices, cooperating with them in making sales. Then you will be glad that you learned your cues by becoming experienced in the role of the apprentice.

Learn Whenever You Buy

Suppose you planned to buy a car, and you knew exactly what make and model you wanted. You wouldn't need a salesman to sell it to you, would you? Supermarket self-service would suffice.

Don't operate that way. Insist that the dealer assign his best salesman to you, and make that salesman "do his stuff." Keep him selling until he has pulled out every trick in his bag.

Take the attitude that you will learn by every available means. Only then will you learn fast. And you will sell fast!

6

The Barrier to Success-
ful Salesmanship

As you read on, you will probably think, "Selling can't be that simple. Karl Bach is holding back his secret methods."

Such, I sense, is the reaction of the audience when I speak to other salesmen about how I sell. There are no miracle techniques. I have no "classified," secret formulas.

I am not versed in psychiatry, and it would be presumptuous for me to go into a discussion of personality problems, but I do know what keeps the average salesman so far below his real potential. I know the great barrier to successful salesmanship.

Many salesmen, without recognizing it, suffer from deep feelings of guilt in selling to a prospect. Why should the salesman feel like that?

You aren't going to exploit your prospect, or steal from him, or malign him in any way. Quite the contrary!

Your service can only benefit your prospect. You are working out ways to give him more money for his family in the form of greater security, the satisfaction of self-provision for his loved ones, self-esteem, and more peace of mind about the future.

Why feel apologetic for the important service you render to your prospect? You are helping him organize his affairs, or you are giving him a keener awareness of his family and business responsibilities and a realistic means of protecting against catastrophe.

Your inner guilt is a symptom of the attitude you entertain toward a prospect. Once you take the position that you are going to trap him and "land" him, you will generate feelings of guilt toward him.

Have a conference—with yourself! First, do you or don't you believe in the true merit of your product? If it has real value and is produced or administered by a principled, reputable company, then you should have no conflict about its true merit.

Second, selling this product can serve to bring its full measure of value to your prospect. It can—provided you study the needs of your prospect honestly and intelligently and then fit your product to his needs. In this way, selling becomes a service, rather than a device to exploit. The fact is that the primary function of selling in its highest form is good service.

In short, have you got a good product and does it offer a genuine value? Or is it a phony? If you think it's a phony, then, of course, you will be "putting one over" on the prospect. This makes for the urgency to make a "quick killing." But none of this is involved in the art of effective salesmanship.

Career selling is based on a long-term view and is developed by building a substantial clientele. Phony products, false claims, misrepresentation, "quick killings"—these are the "delinquents" of the selling business.

You can recognize such feelings of guilt in your very approach to a prospect. There are many signs to warn you. Here are a few:

—You feel overanxious about the interview and have "butterflies in your stomach."

—You enter with a flourish, as if trumpets were sounding a fanfare.

—You produce experts to anesthetize the prospect so you can close him.

—You try for applause instead of sticking to selling.

—You dodge adroitly when he advances a valid objection.

—You don't attempt to close until he seems too weary to resist further.

No one need tell you that such actions are faulty salesmanship. Correct your attitude and you will correct your whole approach to salesmanship.

You are selling a product—a good one, and one you believe in. You won't sell it unless it benefits your client—it must do him good. You hope to build that prospect into a client, then into a repeat client, and eventually into a fruitful source of other potential clients so that you may develop a clientele.

With that kind of attitude, you will eliminate feelings of guilt about selling. And then you will be on your way over the jagged barrier that separates the men from the boys among salesmen.

7

Know Your Merchandise—Know Your Prospect's Merchandise

Generalities are not enough. You must know the basic details of how your merchandise can benefit your client. This means a full knowledge of what you are selling, *plus* learning at least the fundamentals, of your prospect's business.

Here is my favorite story apropos of this point:

Early in my career, one of my prospects was the proprietor of a small retail jewelry store. I knew he needed life insurance, but somehow I could not sell him. I did, however, sell him on the idea of meeting Jerome Breyer, the man who sponsored me in the life insurance business. The prospect gave Jerome a rough time with all the questions he asked. Carefully, I observed Jerome's technique, and mentally made many notes. He concentrated on the jewelry business—talking to the man in his own language. He talked about watches, precious gems, diamonds, gold—and just occasionally did life insurance come into the picture.

The significant lesson I learned here was that to gain a man's confidence, you should be conversant with his business or his work. Then you can talk to him in his own language.

After this profitable experience, I began a cold canvass of every jewelry store in San Francisco. I sold enough to more than justify my effort and time; moreover, I even learned a lot about the jewelry business.

When I exhausted the list of jewelry-store owners, I decided that another line of business should be developed. This time I selected grocery stores.

I called on one owner in this field, but he was always too busy to talk to me. We were constantly interrupted by customers. Here again I decided to bring in Jerome Breyer. I made an early appointment when my prospect would be least occupied. He greeted us at the check-out counter and suggested that we talk to him there. Jerome was quick to clear that with, "Where would you be most comfortable? Let's go into your office or the room in back so that you will not be disturbed."

Asking the prospect for an interview in a place which would offer the most favorable conditions is something I had never attempted. Of course, Jerome succeeded in making a big sale. From this experience I learned another valuable lesson. Don't wait for the perfect situation. It just doesn't come about—not by itself at any rate.

Again, Jerome demonstrated to the grocery store proprietor the benefit of life insurance—in terms of his own business.

Grocery stores are more abundant and closer together than jewelry stores. I made more calls and more sales per week. My income was climbing.

I was encouraged to take a shot at selling bigger policies, —to grocery chain-store managers. With considerable work and very diligent study, I succeeded in selling them too. The same principle prevailed. All I had to find out was how to apply my merchandise to their problems to the best advantage.

8

The Art of Cold Canvass

The Shortest Course of Education in Salesmanship, and the Quickest Way to Meet Prospects

Cold canvass—calling on prospects without advance preparation—is the "cram course" in salesmanship. An apprentice can learn fastest by cold canvass. This was the laboratory in which I tested my sales talks. In the hard school of cold canvass, the more you know about your merchandise the easier it is to succeed. I still believe in and practice cold canvassing, to keep my old sales skills sharpened.

Let's look at an example of cold canvass selling, the door-to-door variety, calling on housewives. This is the "school" I attended in the beginning of my life insurance sales career.

Before ringing the bell, I took a quick look at the house and the grounds. What did it tell me? Were there any signs of young children living here? Did the home suggest that the people were conservative, imaginative, orderly, steady in habits? In short, I "cased" the prospect.

36

As I rang, I stood well back so as not to frighten the housewife when she opened the door.

I said (presenting her with a gift, usually a ball-point pen): "May I give you my business card? I want you to keep it."

HOUSEWIFE: "That's nice." (Reads the ad on pen.) "But we have insurance."

My comment: "I am glad that you do. Have you heard of the latest developments?"

HOUSEWIFE: "Well! And just what are they?"

My cue: "You'll have to help me a bit. In order to bring up-to-date information to you, I must ask a few questions. What is your husband's occupation? How does he spell his name? How old is he?"

HOUSEWIFE: "I'll tell you all of that, but you tell my husband that I asked you not to bother him about insurance."

My retort: "I certainly won't bother him unless I am sure I can be of some service to your family."

His name was Henry Jenkins. He was a plumber. He had a mortgage on his home. His life insurance, taken out before his two children were born, did not name them as beneficiaries.

The first interview at this Jenkins home was possibly my tenth call that day. The first nine could have been complete blanks. But somehow I felt that I had a good prospect here.

In preparation for the evening interview, I did some thinking about plumbers and their needs generally.

The final result: Jenkins became a client and in his train followed a whole troupe of other plumbers.

9

Need Versus Desire

By now it should be clear that I am trying to sell you on the attitude of *never having anything but the benefit of the customer in your mind* when you go into a selling interview.

I have read about men who waited until they didn't have carfare to the poorhouse, and then, overnight, blasted out enough sales to live on Easy Street instead of Skid Row. I know some of these men. Their stories are true and they fascinate me. But destitution doesn't provide suitable conditions for free energy salesmanship.

Each man has a limited amount of fuel which he can convert into free energy for getting his prospects to act. If he is forced to use fuel for combating serious economic and emotional pressures, then he does not have that fuel for energizing his prospects.

For productive living and effective salesmanship, the right attitude is: *Never put yourself under the wrong type of pressure.* Keeping other men's families out of the poorhouse only to become a victim himself—that's not the salesman's destiny. No salesman should be wise in the affairs of other men and a fool in his own.

There is room for the salesman's self-preservation while he is dedicating himself to the preservation of his client's estate.

Keep Your House in Order—Be a Good Financial Housekeeper

Don't accept a drawing account that is so high you will be under stress to meet it.

Don't set a goal so high you will be under stress to reach it.

Don't buy on the installment plan, unless it is the only way to get such necessities as an automobile for your sales calls and a home to live in. Even then, don't make the debt heavier than you can support comfortably.

Don't be reaching out. Everything you need will come to you if you sell well enough to bring it in.

Strain Can Kill Your Chances

Here is another way to see that point.

Take a piece of string in your hands. Pull on it. It has been determined that it will break with a twenty-pound pull. If you are already pulling ten pounds, it has only another ten pounds of resistance remaining.

That is one of the things that happen when you put yourself under stress and then go into an interview. You have only part of your strength left.

A more serious consequence is that the prospect feels your stress too. You are under strain. Your strain communicates itself to the prospect. He does not react favorably to it. He is under enough stresses of his own without becoming involved in yours.

You have either a hard time selling him or else fail to sell him at all. And then, you are under still more stress for the next prospect.

Free your mind of everything but the desire to sell the merchandise that will best benefit the prospect. With such an attitude, you can let the other fellow have most of the "natural aptitudes for salesmanship."

If solidly applied, that attitude alone can make for you a fine income, from free energy personal salesmanship.

10

Men and Mentors

During your selling career, you may meet a few men who have a profound influence on you. I have had the good fortune to meet several such personalities, and they have contributed materially to my growth and advancement.

There is a personal factor involved, of course. The men to whom I responded might not inspire you particularly. You can determine that yourself, but be certain your values are sound. Don't be too quick to disregard a genuine opportunity for some superficial reason. In other words, be objective in your judgment. Remember, too, when a man achieves professional esteem and position, he is worthy of study. If you are lucky enough to come into his orbit, listen to him, give thought to his views and practices, and learn from the ways of a successful man.

Naturally, we must use mature judgment in evaluating these men, but once we recognize their importance and real worth, we should observe them closely and benefit from their counsel.

For want of space, I must limit myself to writing about only a few of the men who played such a significant role in my own selling career.

During my transition period, I advised all my Fuller Brush customers that I was going to sell life insurance.

I had been calling quite regularly at an office where the president's secretary would always show my samples to him. I never did have the occasion or opportunity to meet the president personally, but he never failed to place an order.

When he learned of my new plans to sell insurance, he asked that I come to see him. And I did.

"I am too old to buy life insurance," he said, "but I want to invest in some annuities. I would like to buy from you if I can."

"I appreciate your loyalty, but I don't feel quite prepared to handle annuities without some help," I confessed. "I am certain, however, that in our office we have an expert who specializes in this plan."

The expert turned out to be Walter Robison. I watched him sell those annuities. By the time he had finished guiding the prospect through the maze of possibilities offered by annuities, I realized even more sharply that this was a field for which I was not ready.

Robison also sold the same customer a life insurance policy for his daughter, as a gift to her. So I learned also from this experience that older men could be sold insurance even if they could not personally meet the requirements for life insurance.

No successful salesman is ever a self-made man. During my apprentice period, I opened many sales that I could not close. My sales manager suggested, "Why don't you take Jerome Breyer around with you?"

Jerome, of whom I have spoken before, had the precious faculty of putting everyone at ease the moment he entered a room.

"Sell yourself to the prospect before you try to sell your merchandise—it only takes a minute," he would say.

Jerome would notice immediately what the prospect cherished most in his home or office, and invariably expressed some admiration or appreciation. He didn't become involved in a long discussion—he might have used just a word, and more often only a meaningful glance.

Let's examine that "admire when you enter" technique. You will be a full-fledged journeyman in selling by the time you master this skill, but you begin your training while an apprentice.

Stick to Selling

Don't entrap yourself!

Among my clients are two men, each holding important executive positions with large firms, who have small-scale ship models displayed in their offices.

The models are not intended to provoke attention or discussion. These men simply enjoy looking at them. But I know of salesmen upon salesmen who come in to sell these men and make the same fatal error—they get sidetracked immediately. The salesmen get off to a long talk on ships. Instead of ending up with a sale, they soon find themselves ushered out. Why? Because a quick acknowledgment or an admiring glance at the models will gain far more favor with these men. The salesman who entraps himself by getting involved with the ship models indicates he'll settle for pleasant conversation rather than getting down to the business of the interview.

Babies are one of the most common distractions to salesmen who call on mothers. Admire them, to be sure. But admiring the baby in order to effect a sale is too obvious. Personally, I just glance admiringly at the baby, and mention that I have six of my own. But I get right on with the selling.

My colleague, Jerome Breyer, was an expert closer. I knew a little about closing, for you can't sell Fuller brushes unless you can close sales. But he taught me a great deal more.

In my early experience, I was trying to sell a big partnership insurance case. I made good progress until it came time to ask for the money. Then the partners balked, but I kept the door open.

"There is still some data which I don't have so naturally I can't give it to you," I said. "I would like to bring a man who has all of the information."

I brought Jerome Breyer. In a very short time, we walked out with their check for more than $10,000.

"Why did I fail?" I questioned Jerome. "And why did you succeed?"

"You didn't fail," he reassured me. "There are times when the only way to win is to put in a new pitcher, even though the old one is still throwing well. And I 'won,' if you will, because you kept the gate open so I could get into the ballpark. Never wait until you slam the gate shut before you call for help."

Keep the gate open. Send for the relief pitcher while he can still save the game. You will win many more games that way. And you will pitch enough full games yourself to give you a highly successful season.

Closing is a complex subject. I will discuss it in greater detail later in this book. But the point for the apprentice salesman to grasp at the beginning of his selling career is that *you must start to close when you start to open,* and you must keep trying.

He Made Me a Journeyman

J. Elliot Hall was one of the outstanding life insurance salesmen of all time, before he went into semiretirement in Florida.

I was attending a convention in Miami. I had never met Hall, but I was thoroughly familiar with his work. I telephoned him. He was most cordial and invited me to come and talk with him. The opportunity to talk with a great master like J. Elliot Hall is a rare event.

I had read his sales talks. But hearing the inflections in his voice was a whole new experience. I had heard his lectures. But firing questions, posing as a prospect, and discovering how one of the greatest salesmen managed the tough ones was a thrill that I shall never forget.

Every apprentice should make a point of reading all the sales talks of master salesmen obtainable. But he should do this with imagination. In the printed talk, the prospect's objections are typically routine. The challenge in all this is to imagine how the master would handle the prospect's objections, and how he would employ his resourcefulness in adjusting his answers if the prospect deviated from the stereotyped objections set forth in printed sales material. Better still, the salesman should listen to tape recordings made by the masters of selling.

I talk with a great number of apprentice salesmen. I ask them to sell me. Nearly all of them speak in a lifeless, flat, monotonous voice.

A simple statement, properly emphasized, with the words clearly enunciated and the voice modulated enough to sound interesting, becomes a three-dimensional picture. It takes on "aliveness," flavor and movement. Ten words spoken effectively are worth volumes of dull speeches, in selling.

When I left J. Elliot Hall, I felt ready to graduate to the status of journeyman. He had imbued me with so much enthusiasm for selling and had stimulated so many promising ideas, I was impatient to put some of his words into action upon my return from Miami.

I arranged an appointment with a young physician. Earlier, I had attempted to sell him some insurance, but without success. He was a quiet, retiring individual. Applying the J. Elliot Hall method, I proceeded to fire questions at him. This stimulated his active participation in the discussion and aroused his interest considerably. I made the sale, and here I learned the basic formula of J. Elliot Hall's effective approach.

Hall's masterful technique employed the dramatic use of a series of questions put to the prospect. This stimulated a free flow of ideas between the salesman and the prospect. His questions were carefully thought out so that they would provoke a healthy, lively discussion rather than an argument or antagonism from the prospect. The whole climate of such a discussion with a prospect induces him to *want to buy*. J. Elliot Hall's techniques are so highly regarded that they are included in a number of insurance sales-training programs as well as reference books.

Enormous power in the form of free energy can be released through the use of leading questions by the salesman.

Moving into the Advanced Stage—My Introduction to Estate Planning

A close friend, who was not yet among my clients, suggested I meet Harry Stone, who had guided him so competently in the reorganization of his financial affairs.

At that time, estate planning was completely foreign to

me and what little thought I gave to it was unrelated to the economic problems of people.

When I met Stone, I was immediately intrigued and impressed by his concept of the family. To him, the family was the basic unit in our society, not unlike the corporate entity of business enterprise. As in the case of the corporation, upon the death of the financial head of the family, severe consequences result, most of which could be prevented or at least minimized by advance planning.

In this, I saw a singular opportunity for constructive service to clients generally. I felt, however, that I could not in good conscience extend this service to my clients unless I put the principles into practice myself. My first step, then, was to subject my own financial affairs to a searching examination and have them organized under a comprehensive plan which would best serve the interests of my family.

The fee for Stone's services, although substantial, was the most rewarding expenditure I have ever paid. I added a considerable amount of my own product, life insurance, to my holdings, because it was the most logical step to take at that time. These life insurance holdings became the basis for my own peace of mind.

From that time on, I was a "major leaguer," and estate planning became an extension of the family financial planning I had been working with right along.

The character of my thinking changed. More like an analyst, I was primarily concerned with the "whys" and "hows" of a client's estate, rather than with mere arithmetic. Through economic counseling, and by providing my clients with a blueprint for future action, I was able to offer them greater financial security for their families and themselves.

Once my clients gained an understanding of this concept in dealing with their estates, it diverted their thinking from the price as the primary factor of a policy. Instead they concentrated on the function of insurance and the most efficient way to realize its benefits.

Every salesman is, himself, in search of economic security. If you can make this security possible, through life insurance plans, for your clients, then don't at the same time leave your own future in a precarious state and deny your family adequate insurance protection.

Life insurance is a realistic expression of thoughtfulness. You believe this and convince your clients. Be sure that you exercise the same measure of consideration for your loved ones that you advocate for others. Get some of that precious security you are dispensing—for yourself!

11

S-e-l-l-i-n-g—Only 7 Letters, but What Vistas They Unfold

Give Yourself a Chance

At a meeting of executives, a purchasing agent for one of the important business firms in the country opened his speech with the following statement: "In preparation for this talk, I analyzed the sales approach of the last few hundred salesmen who have called on me. I was appalled to discover that *not one in one hundred gave himself a fair chance to sell me.*"

He continued, "They know they have only a limited time to talk to me. They dissipate that time in asking questions about what I buy, or offering goods I cannot use. They should have been briefed on all this information *before* they called. By the time they determine what to sell me, there is no more time, and they find themselves being ushered out of my office without having given themselves a real chance."

From the housewife to the top executive, there is hardly a buyer who isn't subjected to a procession of salesmen who

49

don't give themselves a chance. Prospects are tired of such salesmen.

You must give yourself a chance!

The next section tells you *how* to give yourself that chance.

One Plus One Equals One

It has been my experience that by working out each step at a time and as though it were a complete entity in itself, I give myself the best possible chance to make a sale. In this way, I keep the whole process at its simplest in my contact with a prospect.

Every interview represents a series of steps. For example, step 1, you must introduce yourself; step 2, introduce your product; etc. The steps can be adjusted according to the individual interview. I discuss this point in more detail later, but now let's direct our attention to giving yourself a chance.

I treat each step as a complete entity, as though it were a sale in itself. I proceed to the next step only after I feel the previous one is a settled issue.

The idea now is to put that first step out of my mind. It is over and done with. The next step becomes a brand new sale, and so is again represented by the figure one.

Nothing can be considered accomplished until the interview is culminated by a sale. And that final closing is once more represented by the figure one.

Thus, I progress from one to one to one—until I reach the final one. And that is the simple explanation of the somewhat perplexing formula: $1 + 1 = 1$.

Let's consider what would happen were I to use a more conventional approach.

I would progress from step one to step two, from step two

to step three, and follow in consecutive order. But a *sales interview is not an automatic machine.* A variety of things can arise. The good salesman must anticipate this and be prepared for sudden changes in his tactics. This means the salesman must be sensitive and flexible. I would not be able to predetermine four steps or seven steps. *You cut down your chances* if you think of an interview in terms of a fixed process with a prescribed schedule or structure.

The point I want to emphasize is to take one step at a time in selling. For example, one step might relate to the needs of the prospect. When that is accomplished, I close the door on that aspect, and go on to whatever step is indicated by the developments in the interview. Thus, the prospect, too, is involved in taking but one step at a time, without being confused or overwhelmed by a barrage of ideas.

Let us study a typical cold-canvass interview to sell insurance. First, consider the conditions of the call. I have an evening appointment with a man at his home. I know very little about him except his name.

Step one: Opening— "Mr. Jones, my name is Karl Bach. May I give you my card?"

At that point, I give him a ball-point pen on which is inscribed my name, address, and slogan: "I don't sell insurance —I help you buy it."

Almost invariably he examines the pen and smiles. His smile closes step one of the interview. I am ready to proceed to the next step.

What has been accomplished thus far? He now knows my name and business, and I have elicited a smile from him. The interview is on. With that type of opening, I can talk *with* him, not at him.

Step one: Opening— "Have you ever seen anything like

this?" I hold up before him a sort of bank book which explains life insurance. I hand him the book. When he takes it and examines it, this step is accomplished.

With that action I have set the stage and established the idea that my business concerns the saving of *his money*. I have taken another step by providing my prospect with a tangible object that characterizes the nature of my business.

Regardless of what you sell, you can hold the attention of a prospect as long as you can get him to *hold and study* some tangible object that symbolizes the value of your product or service. This does not mean, of course, that you will lose your interview if he puts the object down. But it is a distinct advantage to have your prospect study it first. And it helps even more if you can build up the association the object has created.

In essence, two "sales" have been made to move the prospect along into the interview. Now it is time to *challenge* his position. Challenging the prospect is important because it gives you a good chance to sell.

I shall demonstrate how I challenge a prospect.

Step One: "If your bank instituted a new savings plan which would guarantee immediately against the '3 D's' on the money you hope to deposit during your active lifetime, would you be interested?"

This marks your first challenge to him. You offer him a choice between two closes. He can say yes or he can ask, "What are the 3 D's?"

If he questions you about the 3 D's, you tell him they are Death, Disability and Dependency.

A "yes" response moves you into your next step. You can say, "This plan is not easily obtainable. Money alone will not get it for you. You must qualify first. If you are acceptable, it is available to you. If you don't mind doing this for me, I would like to have you qualified by one of our examining doctors."

The prospect's consent to the examination tells you that you are well along the road to the close of the final sale.

"Guts is What Closes Sales"

The old-time salesmen had a phrase—"guts is what closes sales."

Getting the prospect's agreement to the medical examination may require a series of challenges, but getting him to buy is the one challenge you must ultimately win to close a sale.

The "guts" referred to above really means unwavering determination and self-assurance that you will sell your prospect—that you will close this sale.

As with other feelings, this positive attitude in the salesman is communicated to the prospect, and he, too, even if unwittingly, responds with a positive feeling toward buying.

I must caution you to discriminate between self-assurance and overconfidence. Overconfidence will lose, not make, a sale.

Real determination and self-assurance are attitudes, to be sure, but must be demonstrated also by a thorough and carefully thought-out plan of work.

The closing routine is essentially just a routine. You can develop your own; it is just a course of procedure.

Personally, I employ a number of different closing routines according to the nature of the interview and the individual prospect.

In many instances, I simply state—and with genuine sincerity, "Here is the policy. If you entertain any doubts about buying it, I won't let you do so. I don't want you to have it unless "you feel completely certain that it is what you need."

Hit and Run

The prospect has said "yes" and the sale is closed. Now, don't give him reason to vacillate or have misgivings.

In your elation of closing the sale, you might think of one more good thing to say. My advice to you: *Don't say it!*

Nothing is so vulnerable or tender as a freshly closed sale. In your most reassuring and cordial manner, leave immediately. *Don't linger.*

Give the sale time to age and to establish itself. On your next call, you can talk further with the prospect, who is now your client.

12

Seven Words That Can Protect You from Failure

You may have seen these words in sales literature before, but not, I believe, in the same way I use them.

The first five magic words are: WHO, WHY, WHAT, WHERE, and WHEN.

The sixth and seventh are WOW and HOW. I shall discuss these later, but WOW is the big word here.

I put these words to use constantly. They are fundamental to my selling success.

It is the sequence of these words that is important!

WHO — WHY — WHAT — WHERE — WHEN — WOW — HOW.

You give yourself the best chance to sell if you use them in that order.

Who

The principle: *The more I know about a prospect the better chance I have to sell him.*

Who is he? How much do I really know about him?

Who does know him and can tell me more about him?

Who might be mutual friends or acquaintances?

Who can help me approach people who can tell me about him?

What business is my prospect in? Do I know enough about his type of business to talk to him in terms of his work?

What is the level of his personal development? Has he any special training or interests? How much formal education?

Is the prospect married? If so, for how long? Children? How many and what ages? What is his wife like? Does she stay home or go out to work? What kind of work does she do?

What about the prospect's personality? Is he inclined to be conservative or progressive? Retiring or aggressive? Withdrawn or outgoing? Deliberate or impulsive? Ambitious or lacking in initiative? Is he a joiner or an individualist? Any club affiliations?

What can I do to show my appreciation to the people who help me learn more about my prospect? On this point, always reciprocate for a good turn in business. It is a rewarding investment.

Why

The principle: I must be able to analyze the following questions: (1) *Why* should a prospect prefer to buy my product from me, and (2) *why* should he prefer to buy another product from some other salesman? This is basic to effective salesmanship.

I project myself into his position and thinking. If I were in his place and knew all I know about my product, *why* would I buy it? Would I reject it? If so, *why?*

What do I expect from a prospect? Even more important, what should he expect from me? What can he get from others that I cannot offer him? How can I make sure that he derives greater benefit in buying from me than I from selling to him?

Obviously, if I have done my work thoroughly under the aforegoing WHO section, I shouldn't have too much of a problem with providing sound reasons for WHY. If I can't, then I had best revert back to WHO and develop that more completely.

The relation between WHO and WHY is as direct as cause and effect.

In studying my prospect on the basis of WHO, I should have learned his particular insurance needs (immediate and future). Also, I should be able to determine, in a general way, his actual as well as potential earning capacity.

To proceed then to WHY, it is evident that with all of this background on my prospect, I am singularly well equipped to work out an insurance program which is best suited to his needs and interests. Moreover, I can do this within the framework of his present and potential income.

(Let us remember an earlier lesson. If you aren't entirely qualified to handle every phase of the groundwork, be willing to be an apprentice. Call in the expert!)

In the final analysis, then, I can honestly feel that I offer my prospect such a special, personal service, he *should* unquestionably prefer to buy my product from me.

Your WHY may eliminate many prospects. If it does, you might be fortunate. For you will, through this experience, develop the ability to discern a "dead horse" type of prospect.

For your own efficiency, you must sharpen your insight into prospects to recognize whether they are potential clients or hopeless.

Again, let me caution you. Don't be too quick to categorize your prospect as a "dead horse." *You* might possibly be the "dead horse" in this twosome. Examine yourself and your work with a prospect before you determine that the fault lies with him.

The "Old Pro" Versus the Amateur

A big league baseball coach made a profound observation of the basic difference between an "old pro" and an amateur.

He said, "The amateur is always hoping that the ball won't be directed at him; the 'old pro' prays it will come right at him so he can make the right play. The amateur always wants to draw a walk if he can, but the 'old pro' is hoping the pitcher will put that apple where he can get enough wood on it to knock it out of the ballpark. The ordinary man is out of the big leagues in less than three years. The 'old pro' stays on indefinitely; we can't get enough of him. Yet the only difference between the two is *attitude toward the job.*"

The amateur is beset by his anxiety over possible failure. He fears that he will make an error, strike out, or be put out. The "old pro" knows he is likely to make bad plays occasionally, but he wants to get his hands, or his bat, on that ball. This is how he can prove his ability.

Now, I shall demonstrate the "old pro" versus the amateur as it applies to selling.

Amateur thinking: "I just learned he (the prospect) has a friend in the business. I'll never stand a chance. He'll tell me about the friend and close the interview at once."

Old Pro thinking: "If he tells me about his friend, I'll suggest he can always use another friend, and here I am. In fact, I might prove to be an even better friend."

Amateur thinking: "He has a cousin in the business and will probably keep it in the family."

Old Pro thinking: "Many men prefer not to do business with relatives. It is possible, too, that I am more qualified to handle his affairs than his cousin. My job is to work out a plan so desirable to him and sell so effectively that the 'cousin' situation won't be a factor."

Amateur thinking: "His social position and professional status is far beyond mine. I will never be able to speak on his level. He'll never even hear me out."

Old Pro thinking: "My reason for talking with him is neither social nor professional. My business is insurance. I am as qualified to discuss that as he is to discuss his own profession. Furthermore, I'm not competing with him socially or professionally. I just know I can help him."

Amateur thinking: "He is extremely loyal to one of my competitors. I could never break through that association."

Old Pro thinking: "I have a genuine respect for loyalty. I have clients as loyal to me, and I appreciate it. But the market is open. Loyalty does not close the door to better products or better service. I shall present the best plan I can work out for his needs. I shall certainly try to outsell my competitor. That is the basis for healthy competition. After all, it is the prospect's interests that are at stake, not loyalty."

You see, you can rationalize defeat before you start in any area you can name—religion, political affiliation, competition, anything. It is simply a negative approach, and produces negative results.

Why not adopt the attitude of the "old pro"? I have and it pays off. Like the old pro, I want to know what the odds are. I want to know how to maneuver into the strongest position, how to give myself the best advantage in selling. But after that, I want action. I want to get into that interview with all I've got. And when I do, I'll generate free energy to feed that prospect. I'll project myself into the position of the prospect and work out a plan that will give him more benefits than it does me. And I'll close that sale!

What

The principle: Accepting the limitations of my product (as with any product) and the variety of problems which can confront a prospect, I recognize that the "ideal solution" is only rarely possible. Realistically, then, I shall strive to adjust my product to the needs of a prospect in such a way that he will realize maximum benefits with only minimum sacrifices.

No product answers every possible need.

Suppose my product was cars. My prospect needed a car with the capacity of a large trailer; however, his parking facilities would accommodate only a motorcycle.

Obviously, I could not sell him any single piece of merchandise that would meet both of these needs. If I were in the trailer business I would probably offer him my most parkable trailer, and have it equipped with a special carrier for a motorcycle. He could go from town to town in the trailer, park the trailer out of town, and then use the motorcycle. I might have to equip the motorcycle with a compartment to house some of the merchandise he had to take into town.

That solution might be workable, but certainly not ideal. Few ideal solutions exist for the problems of prospects. At best, ideal solutions are a compromise.

I am a salesman. My job is to sell my product. Part of my job is to select and adapt my merchandise so that it approximates the ideal solution. I have studied the prospect, his needs, and his relationship to my merchandise. I am now at the point of selection, the WHAT.

As a salesman, I must be prepared to offer several alternative proposals. Thus I can be equipped to meet the prospect's desires and needs.

The problem of alternatives differs with every line of merchandise. But it almost invariably exists.

If you sell vacuum cleaners and offer but one model, you might have no alternative to worry about—with a prospect who has no vacuum cleaner. You would sell her that one model or nothing at all. But if she did have a vacuum cleaner, you would face at least three possible alternatives: (1) having her trade in the old one, (2) having her keep it, or (3) having her give it to her Aunt Lucy who is always borrowing it anyway.

What alternatives should I have ready for my prospect?

You cannot provide an alternative solution by means of a generalization. You must be specific.

One salesman said, "You should insure your partners against loss in case you die." His general statement about "loss" cost him the sale.

In contrast, another salesman said, "No partner should incur a business debt that might outlive him." The salesman offered specific insurance to cover specific debts. He made the sale.

Service is part of the product, but I must define service before I use the word. Just what service, specifically and in detail, do I intend to give this prospect?

In the life insurance business, service means many things. I must advise the customer and help him and his family. I must keep in touch with him and his affairs to continue my service.

When I deliver my first policy to a new customer, I say, "This policy is only the beginning of our relationship. I shall always be available when you need me. I am no farther away from you than the nearest telephone, regardless of where you might be.

"I will act as watchdog and review your insurance plan from time to time. It is my fond hope that you'll consider me your friend and advisor, and consult with me frequently. I should like to act as a kind of auxiliary counselor in your business and financial planning."

This is my idea of good public relations and how I function all the time. This, even more than technical skill, I feel, is what the public wants most today from salesmen.

If the salesman fails to recognize the importance of good service, he will learn that the prospect will seek out salesmen who make a practice of extending interested and personal service.

In setting forth these concepts, or what I believe constitutes good service, I may be going out on a limb. But isn't that where the fruit is, generally?

Prospect, Customer, Client

It is not unusual to meet a prospect who owns four life insurance policies, sold to him by four different agents.

If the agent who sold him the first policy had known how to develop him into a client, he could have sold the three subsequent policies with a fraction of the effort it took to sell the first one.

This is true because studying the prospect and persuading

him to buy are accomplished in the first sale. And these two steps are the most difficult and time-consuming in the whole selling process.

Clients are far more profitable and require much less time and effort than one-shot customers.

In my business, I must maintain a close watch for changes that may occur in the affairs of a client. Has he married? Has his family increased? Has he been advanced in his job? Or, has he made any other changes that require a different kind or amount of insurance protection? Making certain that he gets that additional protection is part of my service. And service is the mainstay of building clients out of customers.

The future service potential must be incorporated into the original product I sell to a customer. I must not sell him merchandise that will become obsolete when he is ready to buy more insurance. My second sale must be like a sequel to the first. My merchandise must be an integral part of my customer's development. His use of my merchandise must become part of his life, and grow with him. All of this must begin with the very first policy I sell him. I want him as a client. Service must be part of the WHAT that I offer him.

Every American likes happy endings. Give him one and he likes you. Give him a design for living, not for dying. Have I worked out all the happy endings that will come to him if he buys my product?

Have I done everything possible through my product and service to prevent, in the event of my client's death, the dissolution of the greatest corporation on earth—his family?

What does all this mean to a salesman? It means that by making the interests of your prospect the paramount issue in any sale, you will ultimately gain the most favorable chance to sell him.

Where

The principle: *The conditions of an interview should be arranged to provide maximum opportunity to make and close the sale.*

Do I want interruptions? If I don't want them, can I tolerate them? What effect could interruptions have on the interview? Could interruptions ever contribute to an interview? Will interruptions be detrimental to this interview? How can I best avoid them?

If you are an apprentice (and I am still one in many respects), you will find that a free moment to think ahead during the course of the interview (while your prospect is otherwise occupied) is of great value.

Many salesmen get into an interview and then hope for an interruption so that they can do a bit of quick work with their rate books, or find the correct page in the sales manual, or select some appropriate sales literature.

What about the mood of the prospect? If my product concerns his business, is it to my advantage to discuss it at his place of business? If my product is more directly related to his personal life, should I arrange the interview in his home? Would he be more receptive, if I first entertain him at lunch and then talk business? How would he react if I arranged the interview at his club or on the golf course?

Social clubs and golf courses can be highly desirable settings for some salesmen. Personally, I rarely use them. I prefer a business atmosphere for business discussions, where I can generate free energy salesmanship in the interview until I close the sale.

Should those who can exert influence on my prospect be included in the interview? Or is it more advisable to sell him first and then deal with the influencers? How can they help the interview? Or, might they handicap it?

Some husbands have influence over their wives' buying; more often, wives influence husbands.

An influencer might deliberately fight you without realizing he is working against the prospect himself. Also, of course, he can be your ally and fight for you. He can often destroy your sale by using the interview as an arena to exhibit his knowledge. Sometimes, he can bring up questions you wish the prospect would ask.

If the power of the influencer is strong, it might be more expedient to include him in the interview. In this way, you can convince him and the prospect simultaneously; otherwise, you are simply inviting distraction.

Fifty-Step Houses

In San Francisco, it is common for a house to be perched high up a hillside or fronted by a steep flight of stairs. This, to be sure, adds charm and enchantment for the tourist, but it poses problems to the salesman.

While still a rank freshman with Fuller Brush, I would stand before those houses in despair. Laboriously, my eyes would trace the climb to the top. I would deliberate—would it be worth it? I rationalized defeat before I started. One day, I deliberated more carefully and made a dramatic decision. No steps—one or a hundred—would stop Karl Bach!

It was a rewarding decision, for I learned many things about selling through this experience.

Soon, I discovered that if a house had fifty or more steps, I had an almost sure sale awaiting me at the top.

Few salesmen made the climb. The housewives up there were not bothered by a succession of salesmen. Some of these women were so eager to talk to someone, I was often detained.

The other side of that coin was that any salesman who trudged the fifty steps did his darndest to make a sale when he got there. You can be sure, these women met no weak-willed salesmen. They were conditioned to strong selling tactics, as a result. The more inaccessible the location of your prospect, the more free energy salesmanship you'll need. These prospects expect it!

WHERE are *your* fifty-step houses? The customer in some remote area, off the beaten track? The ones in the tough neighborhood where you hesitate even to park your car? Or else, where the traffic is so congested you can't park at all?

The WHERE that makes it tough for the other fellow makes it easier for you.

Do you have any anxiety about the place of interview? Anxiety will work havoc on your selling ability.

Do I know how to get there and how long the trip will take? Have I provided myself with adequate city guides or street maps? Worry about how to find the place, or miscalculating the time needed for the trip, can seriously reduce your effectiveness.

Are there other calls I can arrange in the same vicinity, in case this interview is unduly short, or for some reason the prospect is unavailable?

Always try to insure maximum use of your time. Consolidate appointments in the same area whenever possible. You will find, too, that you reflect far less personal tension in an interview when you've scheduled one or two more appointments preceding or following. This relaxed attitude is very conducive to closing a sale.

You can use each day only once; therefore, every salesman should use it to capacity. A fundamental precept for all salesmen to follow is to cut down on lost motion.

Here is an instance where I converted a defaulted interview into my largest single sale.

The original prospect I called on was unexpectedly called away, thereby canceling my appointment without notice. So I decided to utilize the time by calling on the president of a large corporation. My prospect, in fact, was employed there.

I was amazed to discover that the president was a descendant of one of the most illustrious families in San Francisco. His position and social background did not threaten my self-confidence. In fact, I felt stimulated. I knew that the basic issue involved here was not his heritage or mine. More pertinent was the fact that my product was as useful and practical to him as to any other individual.

Utilizing the canceled appointment constructively was extremely profitable. The happy ending was written up in a six-figure sale.

When

The principle: The same factors that prevail for WHERE must determine the time of an interview. To paraphrase the principle: The time of an interview should be arranged to provide maximum opportunity to make and close the sale.

A nineteen-year-old apprentice salesman, in a last desperate chance to make a sale, called at my office one day at 4:45 p.m. He expected to be ushered right out, I'm sure.

To his astonishment, he found another salesman waiting to see me. He was at least sixty and a veteran in the business.

"Well," the old fellow said with a smile, "there's another man who knows that buyers are always looking for a way to spend that last fifteen minutes. Let's go in and knock him off together."

Both men closed their sales. I, in turn, thanked them for calling at an hour when I was free to see them.

In another case, a young apprentice was told to call upon a buyer whom not even veteran salesmen had been able to interview.

"When, if ever, does he have free time?" he asked the secretary.

"He arrives at 7:00 every morning," she said, "and looks everything over before the others arrive at 8:00."

Promptly at 7:00 the following morning, the young salesman was there.

He had a full forty-five minutes with the buyer before anyone interrupted. That early morning visit netted this young man a $5,000 yearly commission from this client's business.

WHEN will the other salesmen be out of the way so I can see the prospect? Should I call on him on a stormy day when most other salesmen will have taken the day off?

Can I meet him on his commute train and break up the monotony of his daily ride to town? I have sold a lot of insurance to men I met aboard such trains.

If I am to see him at his home, should it be at 8:00 in the evening just after dinner? Or should I wait until 9:00, after his youngsters retire?

If he plays golf or goes fishing, then a sunny Saturday morning could be the *worst* time to call at his home. But, what about a rainy Saturday when his regular plans will be off? He may not know what to do with his time.

"When" Is a Two-Way Street

Up to this point, we have been stressing the WHEN as it applies to the prospect, but what about *you?*

If you approach a scheduled appointment at 8:00 in the morning with fatigue and strain, are you "providing maximum opportunity to make and close the sale"?

Your fatigue may well be the result of a late and tiring business appointment the previous night. You may feel very righteous about how hard you work, but this is poor and inefficient sales planning.

When your energy is at low ebb and you must continue beyond the point of fatigue, you resent that early morning prospect. This is inevitable! And you can't help but communicate this resentment to the prospect. Your patience is easily tried, you are bound to cut corners in your whole sales approach. Is this fair to you or your prospect?

The point here is obvious. If you are working a late appointment in the evening or plan to be late for any other reason, *don't* schedule an early appointment the following morning. On the other hand, if you have scheduled an early morning appointment, don't become involved in heavy plans the night before.

Another question arises. Should you make calls when you have a bad cold or feel ill?

My advice is *don't!* Prospects withdraw immediately and you impose a poor situation on both your prospect and yourself.

"When" Means as Soon as Possible

The more limited your experience, the more work and time is required to process the five steps: WHO—WHY—WHAT—WHERE—and WHEN. As you gain in experience, however, the process will become like a much-used tool— almost automatic.

This might lead you to believe that the advanced salesman can think out his work in a fraction of the time taken by the apprentice. "Work" is the key word here that makes the difference.

As you progress from apprentice to an advanced salesman the nature of your work progresses from relatively simple sales to highly specialized and complex transactions. To prepare yourself for such an interview means hours of careful research, study and thinking.

But never let the preparation time deter you from calling on a prospect. "As soon as possible" defines the WHEN factor, whether you are planning a simple or complex sale.

Set up an early appointment and let that be your deadline. It will serve as a boon to your energy and you will feel compelled to have your preparation accomplished by appointment time. This is valuable discipline.

Before and After

Do you ever start daydreaming about how much money you will make, while the interview is in progress?

I can best illustrate my point by referring to Jim Corbett again. (Remember his motto on "Courage" in Chapter 4.) As you undoubtedly know, he was the light heavyweight who defeated John L. Sullivan and became the world heavyweight champion.

He was relating the story of how he lost his title fight to Jim Jeffries.

"I was way ahead on points," he recalled, "and I got to thinking about the celebrations and all the money I would have. And all of a sudden my back was up against the ropes when I forgot where the ropes were. Next thing was they picked me up from the canvas. It sure was the wrong time to dream."

And I've made Jim's mistake many times early in my career.

Many sales have slipped right out of my hands by my dreaming about the commission instead of concentrating on my prospect and his interests. It's a sure way to lose a sale.

Daydreaming at the right time has its value and can be the very nucleus of future planning and far-reaching goals.

Certainly when I made my way to California many years ago, I dreamed of success, a fine home, and a rewarding life. When I started my insurance selling career, I dreamed of a flourishing business and high esteem in my work. I have no doubt that these dreams inspired me to build toward these goals. Isn't this every American's dream?

The danger is not in daydreaming—even about commissions, if you will—but in dreaming during the course of an interview. It is sheer folly to figure your commission before you've made the sale. Your whole sales approach becomes weak and distorted.

The crux of the problem concerns the WHEN to daydream. *After* you've accomplished your sale, then enjoy the fruits of your labor. Add up your commission and dream!

Wow and How

Have you ever observed how a dynamiter works?

He doesn't ignite his fuse and then start digging the hole. He spends days preparing for the instantaneous explosion that does the work.

The dynamite is the Wow, the one prize pitch that will wipe out all obstacles so that the sale can be closed.

The How is the preparatory work before blasting.

The process of mixing dynamite is frightfully dangerous unless it is done under carefully controlled conditions. A dynamiter who waited until he came to the blasting site before mixing his dynamite would very likely get his head blown off. His death would be almost certain if he used his own homespun ideas about mixing the dynamite. Timing of the blast must be meticulously perfect. There is no room for error. Once it is blasted—that's it!

The same principle applies to Wow.

I prefer to reserve my Wow for the crisis of the interview. Usually this arises during the money discussion. I sense the price objection building up in the prospect's mind, and the problem of finding the money is threatening. That's when I strike with my Wow.

But other salesmen have other ideas—and good ones. Let's study one of them.

I know an insurance salesman who arbitrarily starts on the top floor of a good office-building. He selects a likely-looking prospect in the nearest office and opens, "How would you like to own a policy that pays off to you, if you live, and if you die, your wife gets it?"

If the prospect declines, he goes on to the next office.

That seemingly unimpressive routine has been extremely lucrative for this salesman. In fact, it has provided him with a fine income, a handsome house, and college educations for his children.

Let's see why. How does he open? "How would you like to own a policy . . ." This states his business immediately.

What's next? ". . . that pays off to you, if you live . . ." Here is the Wow! Too many people think of life insurance as death insurance. It's an expense you incur out of love for your family. You, personally, never derive direct benefit from it. Under the proposed plan, if you live, *you* get the money.

"And if you die, your wife gets it." That is the bonus included. When the husband tells his wife he bought some more insurance, he still has the Wow to sell his wife on making the investment.

13

Salesman Showmanship

To be a successful salesman, you must develop acting ability. You study a part, rehearse, and refine your act. In contrast with the theater, your performance is without benefit of prompter or cues, and the applause is extremely restrained.

Your sales talks are the core of your "lines." Commit them to memory. Then dramatize them with skillful showmanship. (I don't mean histrionics!) This is what individualizes even a routine speech.

Showmanship in selling is of primary importance, for it is the art of presentation.

A case in point involves one of my business friends. On her first job out of college she was employed by Marshall Field and Company in Chicago. In her training program with the store, presentation of merchandise was emphasized as one of the fundamental techniques in effective selling.

An artful salesperson can enhance considerably the value of merchandise to a customer by the very manner in which it is presented. To cite a simple example, a moderately priced piece of costume jewelry, placed in a complementary setting and delicately handled like precious jewelry as it is shown to a customer, will immediately command her respect. She may not buy it, but she will be prompted to consider it. In direct contrast, if the jewelry were just placed on the counter in a perfunctory manner, the merchandise would assume no special importance. As a result, the customer would not be stimulated into buying.

The manner of presentation conditions the response of your customer. The more effective your presentation, the more you disarm your customer, and that alone will accomplish half of your selling job.

Always Get Action

Unless the interview indicates no possibility of sale (as some are certain to be), always seek some way to elicit action from your prospect before you leave.

The proverbial "I'll think it over" does not constitute action. You might refer him to one of your other clients as a source of information about you, or suggest he give you the name of some person whose judgment he values so that you can discuss your recommendations with him, before you meet with the prospect again.

The prospect's best form of action, of course, is to *buy* at the time of your initial interview.

Action taken by the prospect demonstrates that he has been energized.

How to Make the Most Use of Each Day

All-day sales meetings are common in the insurance business. Managers conduct workshop sessions for their salesmen to introduce and study new plans or rulings, selling techniques and problems.

Most of my colleagues looked upon the meeting as the day's work. They arranged no other appointments for the day.

This, however, has never been my practice. I always plan appointments en route to the meeting place, and attempt to accomplish at least one successful interview before I arrive.

It has been my observation that most of the other men attending the meeting were somewhat anxious about not producing any business that whole day. They didn't produce any, of course, and as a result found it difficult to devote their full attention to the material of the meeting.

I was able to sit there in the comfortable realization that I had done business before the meeting, or at least had seriously tried. My mind was therefore free and receptive. I could derive the maximum benefit from the session.

En route home, I would similarly schedule appointments if possible. This was particularly profitable, for I could apply what I had learned at the meeting. Creating an opportunity to use my new knowledge while it was yet fresh was enormously valuable. My facility to remember the details was at its best and served to establish them in my memory for future reference.

Frequently I am asked by apprentice salesmen about when in the day is it best to schedule the toughest calls.

There are several different views on this. I know one salesman who sells a Wall Street financial service on a yearly contract basis. Most of his clients renew every year. He always schedules his first call of the day with a client who is certain to renew. Thus, he could start each day with a sale. Opening with a feel of success set up his tone for the rest of the day, and helped make more sales for him.

I find another practice more successful for me. I deliberately set up my toughest calls early in the day. I prefer to use my freshest energies and hours for my hardest battles. This works for me.

You might ask, then, "Don't you go to your office the first thing in the morning and open your mail?" Certainly not! Rarely does a calamity occur if you delay checking your mail until noon. And, I don't see any advantage in cluttering your mind with the attendant problems of mail as you approach your first (and possibly most difficult) interview.

How to Overcome Your Awe of "Big" Men

Do you become overwhelmed by V.I.P.'s? When you have to interview the important executive of a large corporation, do you get stage fright and freeze? Or do you prematurely blurt out your Wow in your haste to make a big impression on the big man?

These are common reactions, especially with young or apprentice salesmen. In true sense, there are no "big" men. What you see here as a big man is simply a little man with big problems and greater needs, both for his business and his family.

Treat your interview with the Very Important Person as you would any other prospect. To you, every prospect must be a Very Important Person. The same laws of behavior apply to all men.

You will observe, however, that the more important a man's position, the more readily he puts you at ease. For he is highly experienced in selling, be they ideas or things. Also, he appreciates the fact that much of the comfort and pleasure in his business and personal life he has bought in one form or another from a salesman. He *wants* to listen to you as long as you do not waste his time. And efficient use of time with a man of importance is the key to your success with him.

His office is usually luxurious in decor and exaggerated in size. The whole operation is such a large-scale affair that you feel miniature. It is this setting, in fact, that more often than not overwhelms you far more than the man himself.

Don't let the trappings distract you when you enter. Get right to the point of the interview.

Don't resort to such time wasters as, "Your valued friend, Thomas C. Jones, president of the Snedley Steel Fabricating Corporation, was kind enough to suggest I present this proposition to you for your consideration."

Your prospect knows exactly who Tom Jones is. More direct would be, "Tom Jones suggested I call on you because I worked out a plan that saved him $60,000. He believes I might do even more for you." This tells him who sent you, introduces the money factor, and accomplishes the first step in the "one-plus-one-equals-one" sequence of my selling process.

Never open with, "Sir, I would like to take a few minutes of your time to present a proposition which . . ." These very words are a waste of time and say nothing in terms of making a sale.

In a classless society such as ours, high-positioned and low-positioned men all share the basic needs of economic security for their loved ones and families. Your work is concerned with developing a plan to protect these interests in the best possible way, whether they are modest or great.

14

On New Ideas

Treat the ideas or techniques discussed in the foregoing chapters quite literally. You will, of course, want to personalize and refine them in your own individual manner.

Adopt the ideas that work well for you, for not all of the devices employed with success by other salesmen will fit well into your natural approach.

I would caution, however, that you give new ideas a reasonable opportunity to work for you. We are all inclined, I believe, to resist new methods somewhat if they fail to demonstrate immediate results. Worse than that, we frequently reject new ideas if we think they will require more effort or careful planning than we have been employing in the past. On this point, I've found apprentice salesmen generally more receptive than "old-timers." Long experience, along with its many values, does have its drawbacks, too. And one of the noticeable characteristics of many men with long years of selling experience is their resistance to change. They relax in their philosophy that "this system has worked fine for me over the past twenty years, so why change now?"

This philosophy is folly. To keep abreast of the rapid changes in living and in working, we must, of necessity, seek new methods to make our selling techniques increasingly effective.

On the other hand, none of us can afford to be indiscriminate. We can't pick up every technique or "gimmick" just because it's new. But here, as with any other aspect of selling, you are expected to exercise mature judgment.

In giving a new idea a "reasonable chance" to work for you, you must fully understand the idea and its purpose. Then, study its relation to your line of merchandise. Does it apply well to your product? How does it suit your general type of customer? If it doesn't appear particularly suitable for all, could you use the idea to advantage in selling *any* of your prospects? If so, then where in your interview structure would this idea have the most impact on your prospect?

Plan out in advance where and how you will use the idea. Then after you have tried out the new idea a few times, evaluate it. If you succeeded in closing a sale, can you ascribe the sale to the new idea? If not, did the new idea contribute in any way? If you failed to close, was the new idea at fault? If not, did it work against the interview in any other way?

You can readily see just how to go about making a fair evaluation of any new idea or technique. You can determine from this suggested process whether to adopt or reject the idea—or possibly only part of the idea, or even the proposed idea with some of your own changes.

Write Your Own Script

In accepting the various techniques and ideas I propose in this book, *always* personalize them in a manner that is natural to *you*. Your selling approach cannot be convincing unless it reflects you and your personality. This is basic to good salesmanship.

You may build the structure of your interview around a dozen of my ideas, but *you* plan your own strategy, *you* create your own speeches, *you* express the ideas in your own individual manner, *you* adjust the ideas to fit your needs, and ultimately it is *you* who makes them work for you. In short, you write your own script!

How can you keep tab on all the techniques that do work well for you? And even those that seem promising.

Keep a workbook. If, after you've "tried and tested" a particular method with good results, write it out. As a ready reference in planning out interviews or sales promotion, you will find such a source invaluable.

Review all the aspects of each interview (successful or not), and particularly analyze what you said and did. Try to determine which techniques or strategies were effective, and which were futile. Note this in your workbook.

In your experience, you'll sometimes find that a special technique or wording in a sales talk suddenly goes well or poorly. Study it out. Go back over the details of your manner, gestures, voice, speech, etc. Note the information for future use.

As with fine actors, good salesmen study and analyze their performances continually. And to extend the analogy, actors devote a good amount of time studying and analyzing the performances of other accomplished actors. The performance of other effective salesmen can provide an extraordinary opportunity to see master-selling methods in action. Avail yourself of every such opportunity.

Listen to Your Prospect

Listen more and talk less. You can miss the best opportunities to close your sale, if you don't let the prospect tell you when he is ready to close. For example:

SALESMAN: "You can make an extra thousand dollars by saving if . . ."

PROSPECT (*interrupting*): "I would like to say that . . ."

SALESMAN: "Just a moment, please. I want to tell you how to make and save that extra thousand dollars, if you will . . ." (*continues for five minutes*)

By this time, the prospect is quite ready to throw the salesman out.

Here is a *good* interview:

SALESMAN: "You can make this extra money if . . ."

The prospect raises his eyebrows. The salesman pauses long enough to let the prospect respond, or better still, to give the salesman the order.

The interview is much like a stage play. You have a cast of two, you and the prospect. Get his participation during the first few minutes of the interview. Keep him in the act and let him play his part.

In the ordinary stage play, the young male lead is called the "juvenile"; the more mature actor is the "heavy."

You play the "heavy" and let the prospect be the hero "juvenile." The experienced old "heavy" usually makes the show.

Let the "juvenile" talk. He will indicate when he is ready to speak. He will probably tell you that you're on the wrong track—there is something important that isn't clear to him.

Listen to *him!* Stop listening to yourself so much. Like the attorney who tries his own case—he has a fool for a client.

Articulate Silence—Silence Is Louder Than Words

Frequently, a prospect will interpose an objection when he can anticipate the salesman's rejoinder.

Here is an example of how *not* to handle this type of situation:

PROSPECT: "Your competitor's price is lower."

SALESMAN (*walking into the trap*): "But when you consider the superior features of my proposition . . ."

PROSPECT (*smiling smugly*): "Your competitor's proposal has all these features and more."

In contrast, here is an effective way to handle this:

PROSPECT: "Your competitor's price is lower."

SALESMAN (*remains silent for a full ten or fifteen seconds, then smiles*): "Here is how I can take care of all your needs and give you peace of mind. For example, this feature could be worth thousands to your family."

Silence will knock down the obvious far better than words. You don't ignore the prospect by silence, you acknowledge his devices by silence.

Here is another *good* interview with this same type of prospect.

PROSPECT: "Your competitor's proposition has several good features which your proposition lacks."

SALESMAN (*looks serious but says absolutely nothing for some ten seconds or more, then speaks with a grave face and a firm voice*): "I agree with you 100 per cent!"

Ten more seconds of silence.

SALESMAN (*with the same grave face and voice*): "I want to show you how I can help you solve a lot of problems and save you money at the same time."

Don't attack your competitors. Your prospect may attempt to test you and try to disparage one of your competitors, even as he does you.

The prospect enjoys the game of pitting one salesman against another. Don't bite! Just sell your own product.

Thinking is hard work. If your prospect will think up your answers for you, give him a respectful ten seconds in which to do it, but then go on. Why should you duplicate the labor of the prospect's thinking?

Should the prospect become sarcastic or offensive, respond with only silence, then be solemn and go on.

Silence can hit hard. But it isn't real silence if you fill it full of a smile that says "we are playing a game and I am going to win."

Be silent the way a high-energy wire is silent. Then, get your free energy salesmanship back at work by throwing the switch.

Reverse Energy

To restate the veteran salesman's maxim, "Sell the prospect. *Don't* let *him* sell *you!*"

In most of us, there is an element of sadism, of wanting to punish another, just to see the other fellow squirm. Often when we are just "kidding" one another, we are manifesting this sadistic desire, but mildly. It comes out strongly when a prospect sells you instead of your selling him.

You can't imbue your prospect with much free energy when he is energizing you right out of your interview.

That "reverse energy" takes a great many forms—the most common one is the "too-smooth" interview.

15

The Interview and Related Aspects

How to Prevent the Too-Smooth Interview from Sliding out of Control

Every experienced salesman recognizes that when the prospect agrees too readily on every issue and eagerly points out all the virtues of the merchandise, the interview is going too smoothly. The salesman becomes suspicious that, in all probability, the sale will not be closed.

A man who intends to buy may appear disinterested, but will also advance objections. The "smoothly acceptive" ever-yes-man is taking the attitude: "Let the salesman ramble on. He is entitled to put on his show. He can't do any harm. I won't buy. Let's be nice to him."

Jolt the too-smooth prospect. Provoke a challenge.

Here, is a *bad* interview (insurance):

SALESMAN: "I can save you an extra $1,000."

PROSPECT: "Wonderful! In fact, I can see that it might be $1,500."

In contrast, here is a *good* interview:

SALESMAN: "I can save you an extra $1,000."

PROSPECT: "Wonderful! In fact, I can see that it might be $1,500."

SALESMAN: "In that case, let's take immediate steps to determine if you can qualify. I cannot know the best plan for you until I find out how you qualify. Let's follow through right now."

Everyone can close on a minor point which will then lead to closing in on the big one.

The too-smooth interview is not limited to new prospects. You will find that the firmly established client can play the game, too.

A chemical manufacturer's representative was showing his local distributor how he could increase his business by 5,000 cases a year through proper merchandising methods with a new product.

The distributor, however, was quite happy with his present volume of business. More volume meant adding more salesmen. He wasn't particularly enthusiastic about expanding his staff, so he was just acting politely agreeable.

Abruptly, the salesman rose, grasped the edge of the distributor's desk, leaned over and glared directly at him.

"Do you mean that you are agreeing with everything and buying nothing?" he shouted. "Do you realize what you are telling me? That if I want to grow in this territory, I've got to get myself a new distributor."

It was, of course, an act. The distributor was too well established. To eliminate him would have been major surgery; the salesman had no intention of acquiring a new distributor for the line.

All of this the distributor knew. But the salesman was acting out the role of a salesman. The distributor was jolted. He took on the new line.

The greatest blow to my ego is to have the prospect label me as a great salesman, but fail to buy even a token order from me. The word *salesman,* to me, means just that—a man who sells.

Prevent Postponements of Action

At some point in almost every good interview, especially if you are trying to sell the prospect all that he ought to buy, he will attempt to postpone the action.

If the prospect succeeds in postponement, on your next call he will try to sell you on his complete refusal to buy. Postponements rarely work to the salesman's advantage. On the second call, the prospect may genuinely fail to recall what he had agreed to during the "one-plus-one-equals-one" development of your original interview.

I have always functioned in the belief that people are good, honest and sincere. I take that belief into every interview with me. In my experience, I've encountered relatively few people who were basically dishonest or insincere—possibly because I am not predisposed to look for dishonesty. I contend that if you really think "good," you ordinarily invite "good."

I assume that when a man asks for a postponement, he believes that we will work out a better deal in the future. And if, at the second interview he forgets what was said at the first one, I believe he really doesn't remember.

Frequently, any of us will rearrange the facts of the past as we recreate them in our memories. We slant them to favor ourselves.

Often, however, the prospect's memory is reliable, and I can pick up the postponed interview at the very point it was broken off, but I prefer not to take that chance.

So, when he says, "Let's wait," I test him. I want to ascertain if there is a real basis for delaying the decision or if he is simply procrastinating.

Here is a *bad* interview:

PROSPECT: "Let's think this over for a while."

SALESMAN: "I'm sorry to hear you say that. We know what we agree on. Can't we settle it right now?"

Here is a *good* interview:

PROSPECT: "Let's think it over. Phone me in a day or so."

SALESMAN: "I'm glad you brought that up. Why don't we think about it together, right now? Apparently, some objection or question is still in the back of your mind, and I want to help you clarify whatever is still in question. We'll satisfy that doubt, whatever it may be, and then we'll deal with it *together*. May we?"

Here I am making a "one" sale in the "one-plus-one-equals-one" process. The sale is in the word *together*. I go right on with my interview, but with more emphasis on listening than talking. I want to give the prospect every opportunity to disclose what is on his mind. We find this out *together*. We do not separate while he, alone, thinks through an issue about which I am thoroughly familiar. I can render my best help to him if I am *with* him.

How to Roll with the Punch When the Prospect Says "Wait a Few Days"

Sometimes the prospect's wish to wait a few days is admittedly legitimate. And very often, the situation is the salesman's own fault. Here are examples:

PROSPECT: "I must discuss all such propositions with my partner."

Clearly, the salesman has failed to plan his WHERE and

WHEN properly. He should have scheduled the interview WHERE and WHEN the partners could be interviewed together. None of us can bat 1,000 in projecting our interview plans, but we can raise a 200 average to 300 if we strike out less.

PROSPECT: "I want to talk it over with my wife."

Again, the proper planning of the WHERE and WHEN might have precluded the delay.

PROSPECT: "We are in full swing of the peak production season. I can't do a thing right now."

Here, the WHEN is ill-timed.

PROSPECT: "We are in the process of making major changes in our production system." (Or, "in our methods, financial setup," etc.) "Last year your proposition would have interested me. Now, we must wait until all the changes have been accomplished."

The WHY and WHAT should have been considered in relation to the anticipated changes *before* the interview. Possibly even the WHO was also incompletely studied. The salesman should have been aware of the prospect's thinking.

When you are hit by a legitimate "wait a few days,"—roll with the punch by closing on a minor point. Your minor point must be one that will *definitely certify* that a sale is in process. It must be a positive step in your "one-plus-one-equals-one" formula.

Here is a *bad* interview:

PROSPECT: "I must wait because . . ."

SALESMAN: "I can see your point, so why don't I call back in about six weeks and . . ."

Here is a *good* interview:

PROSPECT: "I must talk this over with my partner. He will be out of town for the next two weeks."

SALESMAN: "Good. In the meantime, why not take your

physical examination so that we have that established when we discuss the plan *together* with your partner?"

Here is an interview that often produces good results:

PROSPECT: "I must talk it over with my partner (wife, etc.)."

SALESMAN: "I have no doubt that you can explain everything that we have discussed clearly to him (or her), but our field has a lot of angles to it. We haven't covered them all. Your partner might query some point that would be unfamiliar to you. I would like to be on hand to help explain such questions that could arise. Let's make a date for us to get together with your partner."

Note the approach of the salesman: *You and I have become allies in making this sale* and *you are making the decision for both of us* on how I shall handle the problem of answering new questions that might be raised by your partner.

When you call on the partner, you will then have your WHO — WHY — WHAT — WHERE — WHEN — WOW — HOW processing to do with him. You'll need information about him. Right before you is one of the most reliable sources of that information—his partner. But you should tap other sources, too.

On one occasion, a prospect said to me, "This must be cleared with my wife."

We arranged that I call on his wife the following Tuesday morning. He told me that she had been a private secretary to the vice-president of an oil company at one time.

I knew that vice-president and contacted him. In the course of our conversation, I gained very useful background information about his former secretary.

When I met the prospect's wife, I talked a bit about various men whom I had sold in oil companies, and referred particularly to my acquaintance with her former employer.

In trying to sell her, I took the position: "I feel fortunate that she has been well trained in business, that her family means everything to her, and my proposal is a sound business transaction for the best interest of her family." The sale was closed.

It's Human to Err, but It Can Be Costly

The most a pitcher can get "on" a batter is two strikes and three balls, a total of five, before something has to happen. You would assume that a smart man could add up to five just by counting on his fingers, wouldn't you? Yet the baseball umpire holds in his hand an indicator to count the balls, strikes and outs as they occur.

Under pressure, any man can forget the simplest figures, or even miscalculate them. It is to prevent this that the umpire uses his indicator.

Mishandle the figures in an interview, and the prospect who is trying to sell you will have you over a barrel. He will laugh you out of all chance to sell. And, all interviewing is under the kind of pressure that is conducive to miscalculating or committing an error.

There is something impressive about being exact and careful about your figures. It is part of your job as a salesman.

In my office, where I conduct most of my advanced and complex interviews, I have a new and efficient electrical computing machine. I turn from my prospect and compute some figures on that machine. It makes sales for me.

Some salesmen use slide rules or pocket adding machines in the presence of the prospect. If they serve as an auxiliary to making a sale, they should be part of your selling routine. I don't use these props. To me, the general manner in which a man approaches his selling is more important than the specific tools he uses.

Figures are focal points. They can distract the prospect from trying to sell you and direct his attention to your interview. Make an act of using them, but accuracy is essential. Remember, however, that even the most accurate figures will not ultimately sell your merchandise—ideas must precede arithmetic.

Some Power or Color Expressions and How to Use Them

A "power expression" is a word, phrase, or expression that uses drama to add energy to the interview, even when the prospect recognizes its purpose.

Don't hesitate to use power expressions. The prospect expects them, and for him it is part of the flavor of the interview. But it works. Like everything else in a sales talk, however, the power expression must be true and convincing. When true, it is able to take the prospect back into the interview when *he* has been trying to sell *you.*

Here is a *good* interview:

SALESMAN: "I can't sell you this product; I can only help you buy it. *You are in the driver's seat.*"

PROSPECT: "I don't want your physical examination. I'd rather use the $200 premium to bet on the horses."

SALESMAN: "The horses? *Wouldn't you like to know whether or not my company would bet on you?*"

PROSPECT: "I can't listen to all of that stuff."

SALESMAN: "Selling is like teaching. If I can't sell you, then I am making it easy for the next man in my line who tries to sell you."

PROSPECT: "I prefer to spend my money on good living right now."

SALESMAN: *"The art of good living involves freedom from worry about the future.* My job is to help you achieve that freedom."

PROSPECT: "I am a successful man. You should try selling this to an unsuccessful man. He needs it more."

SALESMAN: "Success means realizing your full potential. I am here to show you one of the ways to live up to greater capacity."

PROSPECT: "I have friends in your business."

SALESMAN: *"You can always use another friend,* and here I am."

PROSPECT: "I want term insurance. It's cheaper."

SALESMAN: *"You don't want to pay alimony, do you?* Well, alimony is a live man's cash surrender value, and term insurance is just a dead man's alimony."

PROSPECT: "You are pushing me too hard. Your competitors go easy. Why don't you?"

SALESMAN: *"I notice that you didn't buy from them, did you?* I can be just as easy on you, but I prefer to make it easy for your family by giving them the benefit of my product."

These expressions won't close a sale, but they will energize the prospect and get the interview over a hurdle. They won't get the car to its destination and park it there, but they will release the brakes and shift the gears into high. Close every interview on some kind of definite decision, if only to keep the door open for another chance later on.

Power expressions count only when the emphasis is on *power*. Don't be afraid to alienate the prospect's affections through the use of a barbed phrase. There will surely be a reconciliation after you have sold him.

It's better to be respected by a client than to be liked by a prospect who didn't buy.

Simplicity Speeds Your Selling

Keep your approach simple and you'll keep it salable. Anything that complicates an interview will slow it down; in fact, it can defeat it entirely. Sell when you sell. Avoid impediments.

The tendency to clutter up the interview stems from your desire to be an actor. Many actors have a propensity for being "hams"; that is, they try to recite *Hamlet* on any and all occasions. Discipline yourself to confine the "soliloquy" to a formal role in a stage performance. In the succeeding section, we will look at some of these impediments.

Jokes in the Interview

I rarely tell jokes during an interview. I open and close with pleasantries, but as a rule, I don't introduce humor into an interview. Possibly I avoid jokes because I neither remember them nor tell them well, but I believe if they really contributed to my selling, I'd soon learn to handle them. Some salesmen make good use of jokes in their interviews. If you are one of them, then here are some principles to observe:

Keep it as brief as you can.

Make sure that it illustrates a point that is immediately at hand.

Don't let it invite the prospect to tell *his* joke in return.

Keep it as clean as you can and avoid vulgarity. Never get bawdy for the sake of being bawdy. This is no achievement.

There is no joke that can't be made suggestive or obscene and there's hardly a joke that hasn't been.

Let's look at a *good* interview.

PROSPECT: "Every salesman who comes in here starts in by telling me how wonderful I am, how well I qualify, and I don't like flattery."

SALESMAN: "The old billy goat said to the young nanny goat, 'You look beautiful to me.'

"She answered, 'No kidding.' (*Pause for laughter, if any.*)

"I'm not going to try to kid you for a minute. Salesmanship is a serious business to me."

Here is a *bad* interview:

PROSPECT: "Every salesman flatters . . ."

SALESMAN: "An old billy goat who stunk like - - - - - walked up to a sweet young nanny goat and said, 'The boss says you smell like an - - - - - but to me you seem sweet and beautiful.'

"She answered, 'You can't kid me, you old - - - - -, I don't want no kids.'—Ha! Ha! Ha!"

PROSPECT: "That reminds me of the traveling salesman who. . . ."

Let's analyze that interview.

The salesman, trying to monopolize the stage as long as he could, dragged out that joke *ad nauseam. He can hold the attention of the prospect for only a limited time. He has dissipated much of that time.*

Resenting the attitude of the prospect and perhaps harboring other resentments, the salesman has worked out his antagonisms by resorting to all the profanity and vulgarity he could get into the story. His interview was reduced to its basest level. Only high-level interviews produce high results.

The prospect has launched into the telling of *his* story. The salesman is obliged to laugh whether it is funny or not. *The prospect is now selling the salesman.* The salesman sold the prospect on listening to a story, and in all likelihood this is the only sale he will accomplish in the whole interview.

Here is how I might have handled that interview:

PROSPECT: "Everybody flatters me . . ."

SALESMAN: "I don't flatter anyone. Let me show you the figures and let them speak for themselves."

I would play the part of the salesman. I would play it straight, without doubling as comedian. I would sell the prospect on playing his role as a *preferred* prospect: "one plus one equals one."

Some proficient salesmen use jokes in their interviews. If you find they contribute to your selling, then use them. But observe the principles: brevity, applicability, and wholesomeness.

I have known some men who became so preoccupied with the jokes they were going to tell the prospect, they forgot to plan the sale.

Jokes are a side show. The sale itself is the main feature. Never let the side shows eclipse the feature performance.

Slang in the Interview

I never use slang in an interview unless and until the expression has established itself as a valid part of the American language. I don't pick up the latest cute expressions from television or comic strips.

Current slang breaks the flow of energy and is a force of distraction. I want my prospect to think of my merchandise and not of the comic strips. For that purpose, simple and accepted English is far more effective than slang.

The Use of Technical Terms in an Interview

If the prospect is unfamiliar with a technical term, its use only confuses him. When you and the prospect are completely familiar with a technical term, then it is expedient to use it.

Two physicians will discuss a case in medical terminology. Each has had long years of training, most of which was devoted to learning exactly what the terms mean. If you are in the position of the physician, and your prospect is equally conversant with the subject, then use your technical terminology. Otherwise, avoid it. Employ simple, easily understood language; it sells.

Here is a *bad* interview:

SALESMAN (*to prospect who is untrained in insurance jargon*): "In the non-forfeiture provisions and the settlement options, this policy is . . ."

PROSPECT (*interrupting*): "Provisions are what I used to be fed in the army, and in the settlement where I used to live we had no options."

SALESMAN: "You don't understand. The non-forfeiture provisions are a table of cash and loan values, paid-up insurance values, extended term insurance. Under the settlement options the widow or you can get a variation of types of . . ."

PROSPECT (*aloud*): "You are right. I don't understand." (*Silently to himself:* "And I'm not sure that you do either."

Here is a *good* interview:

SALESMAN: "This policy is not a coupon that your relatives redeem for cash after you die. Should you ever need money, the policy has loan values so you can borrow on it or even, if necessary, you can stop paying premiums and take paid-up insurance values. This would still leave some money to your family.

"Or you could convert the policy into temporary insurance for a few years without further premium outlays. It offers many ways in which your widow or you can take the money when it falls due, too."

PROSPECT: "Is there a technical name for all that?"

SALESMAN: "Yes. It is called 'non-forfeiture provisions and settlement options,' but let's concentrate on what it will do for you. That's the important meaning for you."

Often the salesman flaunts technical terms to impress the prospect. He holds the center of the stage with them. He thinks they make him sound professional.

Don't concern yourself with superficial ways of impressing your prospect or gaining prestige through these means. If you succeed in giving your prospect a plan that will serve his best interests and protect him and his family against catastrophe, you will impress him—and justifiably!

On Giving Advice to Prospects

Unless your advice applies directly to what you sell, giving it puts you in the center of the stage, but only at the cost of effective salesmanship.

Don't offer advice when it does not concern the sale of your product. If the advice is good, you gain nothing; if bad, you lose the good will of your prospect.

There are enough problems directly related to your product and your prospect to handle in the interview. Don't compound them by venturing into outside areas.

If your prospect makes a point of seeking advice on some problem not related to your product, then refer him to a good authority in the particular field involved. You must be courteous and accommodating, if possible, but don't get sidetracked from the main business at hand—your selling your product to him.

On Personal Attire and Appearance

Your personal appearance is highly important, but when it becomes an issue (positively or negatively), it replaces the issue of the sale itself. You will be "selling" your clothes instead of your product.

If your attire is inappropriate for business, the attention of your prospect will be misdirected. He'll be giving all or part of his attention to how you look instead of what you're selling.

How should you dress for selling? Generally, it is desirable to be conservative in your choice of clothes. You will find that when your style of dress is restrained, you are always in good taste. You, then, are prepared to meet with any prospect, whether he is in modest circumstances or holding an important executive position.

Just as silence is an important value in effective salesmanship, so, too, is dress that is quiet. When my voice is silent, I don't want my clothes to start talking.

Your attire should be in keeping with your work. When you tell a prospect: "I have a plan that can save you $50,000 over the next twenty years," you can't look like fifty cents yourself. On the other hand, don't try to look like $50,000 either. It is too incongruous and you can't sound convincing when you don't look convincing.

Personal grooming is at least as important as the choice of clothes. Obviously, you can't hope to make a favorable impression on anyone if you show personal negligence. Dirty hands and nails, the need of a shave or haircut, soiled clothing, lack of fastidiousness about your person—all make very poor impressions. How can a prospect feel confident that you will handle his affairs in an orderly and careful manner when you appear so poorly organized yourself? How can you command the respect or trust of a prospect, when you lack the self-respect and dignity to present yourself well?

The Suspicious Prospect

If your prospect entertains any apprehension about you or your motives, you are defeated before you start. You must, therefore, immediately dispel any kind of suspicion in your prospect.

Here is an example of one of my own experiences and how I precluded any suspicion of my motives with a young woman prospect.

For quite some time, I noticed a fine-looking young woman come into the same coffee shop I frequented. In talking to the proprietor, I learned that she was an executive secretary. Her whole appearance suggested that she was a good, substantial type of person—an ideal prospect.

One day I approached her, saying, "Will you join me at a cup of coffee? I have an idea I would like to discuss with you."

She agreed. I promptly spoke of one of my sons, and showed her a picture of my children. *That dissipated all suspicion* that I might be trying to "pick her up."

I opened by selling. "We have an unusual plan particularly designed for a girl like you. You probably *have no plan for making your present income work for your future.*"

In keeping with my usual routine, I presented one of my ball-point pens, which indicates on it that I am in the insurance business. *That dispelled all suspicion* that I might be trying to keep the nature of my business "up my sleeve" until she was "hooked."

"I've done nothing about future income," she said, "and I just got a $50 a month increase."

"Put half of it into your future," I said, and elaborated more fully on the plan.

Doesn't that sound simple? Note that I had developed the WHO—WHY—WHERE—WHAT—WHEN process. No real WOW was needed. But the HOW had been worked out carefully in detail.

The final arrangements were worked out during an interview in my office. She bought disability income insurance and retirement income life insurance.

She was so pleased that she was instrumental in introducing her employer to me. He, of course, offered far greater possibilities as a prospect.

The whole interview, however, might have been fruitless if I had not deliberately taken steps to preclude all possibility of suspicion immediately.

Objections Are Good for an Interview

In free energy selling, you may have to provoke objections from your prospect. Otherwise, the interview becomes hidebound and rigid.

Here is an example:

The prospect was a store owner. He took one of my ball-point pens and upon reading my name and business on it, remarked, "No man can sell me any life insurance."

That was my cue for low speed ahead.

"Would you like your son to own a bigger store than this one?" I asked.

"Yes, but I don't think he ever will, what with taxes, etc."

"Would you buy him a bigger store than this if the down payment were only $500? With that down payment, would you buy it if you were certain that the purchase price would come to your son tax-free, if you should die before you finished the payments?"

Note how the reference to his present business caused him to make the objection about a bigger one, because of taxes.

The principle is clear. Cause him to object. When you know his real objections, then free energy salesmanship can energize him out of it.

Salesman-Prospect Relationships

If possible, don't fraternize with your prospect. Avoid, if you can, too personal a relationship.

It is difficult to do business with close friends, because too many irrelevant personal factors are introduced into the interview. These clutter up the discussion and, as a consequence, neither you nor the prospect can realize the maximum benefits of the interview.

Also, in becoming too friendly with a prospect, you invite other problems. You cannot be objective in evaluating your prospect and his needs. You become emotionally involved and this interferes with your whole selling approach. Obviously, you cannot exercise the same control over any part of the interview as you do in a purely business relationship.

In short, always try to preclude or eliminate everything extraneous—whether it is digression, distraction, or personal involvement. These factors become serious obstacles to effective salesmanship. Separate your business from your personal life. This is a case where your business and pleasure lives should not be mixed.

16

Sidelights on the Interview

The Opening

The structure of a sales interview is defined but completely flexible. To produce sales, you must handle each interview with the utmost sensitivity to your prospect and make continuous adjustments.

Before you meet with the prospect you plan out your interview: your opening, the development, and the close. The plan, however, is only the general framework.

While you are in the actual interview, your awareness must be sharp enough to sense in an instant the ripe moment for closing the sale. And that moment may even arise at the opening of the interview. Should you proceed with the prepared plan, no matter? Certainly not! The time to close a sale is entirely contingent upon that "ripe moment." Whenever it occurs—at the opening, an hour later or even a week later, you must be ready to close then and there. The closed sale, after all, is your ultimate purpose for the interview.

Your opening can set the whole feeling tone of the interview and should accomplish several things. It should tell the prospect (*a*) who you are and what you do and (*b*) why you are there.

Often (*a*) will accomplish (*b*) as well. When, for example, I introduce myself as an insurance company representative, the prospect learns immediately that my reason for seeing him is to sell insurance. Always be direct about your ultimate objective: to make a sale.

In addition, your opening should (*c*) elicit from your prospect a cordial and receptive response. Don't encourage an overly friendly mood, however. You don't want him to say, "You are too good a friend to try to sell me anything."

And, finally, your opening should induce the prospect's participation in the interview. He is not a neutral observer—an onlooker. He must take an active part.

Below is one way to handle the problem pointed out in (*c*). It was used by a business friend of mine who is a master salesman of imported goods.

PROSPECT: "I can see that you are too nice a friend to try to sell me anything."

SALESMAN: "Then shake hands with your worst enemy!"

Never delay getting the prospect started in playing his part.

The Power Opening Is the "Break Loose"

When a locomotive starts a long freight train moving, the amount of power needed to "break loose" the bearings and bring it up to speed may be ten times that needed to keep it rolling after the speed has been produced.

A parallel situation exists in sales interviews. You must have that "break loose" power to generate your interview so it will "get rolling." The need for the "break loose" is the reason you start your car in low gear.

Here is an example of my usual opening statement: "Here is my business card. I want you to keep it, but not in your wastebasket."

With that, I present one of my pens upon which, you remember, is inscribed my name, address and slogan: "I don't sell insurance. I help you buy it."

As the prospect reads this, I add: "I sell lifeboats."

Then I pause and wait for his response.

This, briefly but instantly, connects the prospect to the free energy, the power, that is to energize the interview. It is not merely an introduction. It is a *power* opening!

In direct contrast, here is the type of opening that is completely devoid of "power"; in fact, it is "power in reverse." It will never get "rolling" and will only antagonize the prospect from the very start.

SALESMAN: "I represent the Blank Company and we have a proposition which, if you will, sir, kindly give me a few minutes of your valuable time, I am sure you will find of great benefit to you. Does that interest you? I am sure that it does. Our proposition is . . ."

The power opening must be brief, provocative, and mildly amusing. It must give the prospect a *mental concept of what your merchandise will do for him.*

Note that in the example of my own usual opening, life insurance can be compared to a lifeboat. Life insurance has saved many families from financial shipwreck. It has enabled many men who lived too long, and many widows whose breadwinners have passed on too soon, to get aboard another ship and start a new course. The uncertainty of life's span and the certainty of death have built the giant institution that is life insurance.

Your power opening, whenever you sell, must depict what it does for the prospect:

(a) Money for future delivery to you or your family.

(b) More mileage for your premium dollar.

(c) Peace of mind when you take care of the three D's: Death, Disability and Dependency.

(d) Spare tires on the highway of life.

These only suggest the endless variety of such "picture" power openings.

Don't Prejudge the Action of Your Prospect

Big league ballplayers in the field shift with every batter. Watch closely, and you'll see that they also read the catcher's sign and shift slightly, or else lean toward the spot where that batter is apt to hit the pitch that is coming up. But with all of that, they are constantly on the alert and ready for any eventuality.

They know how to shift because they have studied the WHO of that batter. They know which way to lean because they know the HOW of that pitch. You, in an interview, are the pitcher, the infield and outfield. And like them, you can't prejudge. You must be prepared for any action.

Open your ears in readiness. When you open your mouth, you often close your mind. Salesmen who talk too much are usually too shortsighted to see the sales potential in clear view of a wider range of vision.

Don't make speeches to your prospect. Encourage his talking throughout the interview. If there could be a formula for the opening it would be: Mild amusement plus mental picture plus simplicity plus brevity plus sincerity plus silence equals Success. When the prospect hits your pitch, you have to determine in an instant whether to continue with mild humor, to begin all over again, or to become serious at once.

Little Gifts Can Open Eyes Wide

As a child in Germany, I was always intrigued by the various salesmen who came to call on my father. He was in the meat and sausage processing business. One of these salesmen —he sold meat spices—always remembered to bring a small gift for each of us children every time he called on my father. We looked forward to his visits and told our father how much we liked him. This was shrewd salesmanship, for he got most of my father's spice business.

When I was selling Fuller brushes a number of years ago, the popular gift brush—it is almost the trademark of Fuller salesmen—seemed the most natural thing in the world to me.

In the life insurance business, I have always continued the practice of presenting a gift. I use it in some manner, with whatever I might sell and in any market. It works.

There is, however, a fine line that must not be crossed. You must heed the demarcation that distinguishes a gift from a bribe.

Ordinarily, gift "handouts" are for the opening. (I don't confine my gift giving to just the opening of an interview, but I shall discuss that later.) Every giveaway I use carries my name, address and slogan: "I don't sell insurance, I help you buy it." It would be of little value without my full identity.

For example, I give out plastic bottle caps for carbonated beverages. Imprinted on each one is: "You're tops with Karl Bach."

I have used dozens of different giveaway premiums. I bought them from salesmen who gave me many new selling ideas.

Some of my little gifts include:

- a dainty clothes brush that fits in milady's purse and slides in and out of its own plastic case
- a plastic abrasive nail file
- a transparent plastic coin or token carrier that fits into a small purse or pocket (mighty handy for parking)
- a combination bookmark–magnifying glass, imprinted with: "So you *can* read the fine print on your policies" (I advise clients to do just that. "Too often the big print giveth, but the small print taketh away.")
- a ten-way card or photograph holder—holds photographs or identification cards in full view and fits neatly in purse or pocket
- a letter opener
- a small strand of simulated pearls in heart-shaped gift case (to encourage little girls to absent themselves from the interview)
- a short, combined ball-point pen and phone dialer (ideal for use at telephone and keeping my phone number at hand)

I use many more, and each item serves to identify me, my business and location.

Cast Bread upon the Waters

You never know the results little gifts might yield, but more often than not, they are like the proverbial "bread cast upon the waters."

One day I called on a prospect at his home. I knew that he had no children so all I brought were my personalized ball-point pens.

When I arrived, however, I found several neighborhood children there. I promptly presented a pen to each one. I closed the sale.

A few days later, I received a phone call from one of the parents of these children. My pen had served, effectively, to introduce me and my business. I called on this family, and sold them as well.

I have a friend who sells power transmission equipment for use in factories. He gives desk thermometers as gifts. They are more expensive than my pens, but his individual sales are large enough so that the more costly gift does not seem out of line. He can trace several sales to men who upon visiting those factories, noticed the thermometers. They would admire the thermometer and note down the name and address of the salesman.

If you give at all, give generously and willingly. Any suggestion that you are niggardly with your gifts will work against you.

I had occasion to call at the office of a large company one day. When the receptionist asked for my card, I gave her a "Bach special" pen. She proceeded to hand it to an office boy to take into the boss. I stopped him immediately.

"Wait a minute," I said. "How many people handle a business card before it reaches the boss?"

"Four," she informed me, "including me, the office boy, the secretary to the boss, and, of course, the boss himself."

I then gave the office boy three more pens, and told him to distribute them, but be sure the last one was brought to the boss.

My "card" reached the boss quickly and he came out at once. The value of the "waiting in the office" time that I saved was worth many times the cost of the pens.

Do it one way or the other. Either give no gifts at all or else make it "every day is Christmas when I make sales calls."

The Golden Egg

One day, I took a fancy to a toy goose I saw in a shop. The little goose would lay a golden egg when squeezed. I promptly bought it to bring home to one of my children and just tucked it in my pocket.

That same day, I called on a prospect en route home.

I was greeted by his wife: "I know who you are and what you sell, but I don't want my husband to spend the money."

I walked in, sat down, and put the little toy goose on her table. I remained silent as I squeezed it so it would lay a golden egg. She watched the performance somewhat apprehensively, but also amused.

"If you owned a goose," I asked, "that would lay 50,000 golden eggs during the next twenty years, you would insure that goose for full value, wouldn't you?"

She responded immediately: "You bet your life I would!"

I looked at her meaningfully, "Your husband is that goose."

"You win!" she said with a smile. "I'll see to it that he does buy."

Elementary, perhaps, but such "gimmicks" have laid many golden eggs for me.

Difficult Cases Require an "Or Else!"

When you sell a product that is a concrete object, like a Fuller brush, an automobile, or a beautifully engraved life insurance policy, it is sometimes good selling strategy to take it back from the prospect after a short time, if he doesn't pay for it.

This technique is often effective in cases that are difficult to close. In this way, the prospect realizes that he cannot own the product unless he pays for it. He must spend the money, "or else!"

The problem of money is the most common excuse for not buying. Review the major points quickly. Use your WOW. Make the cost seem minimal as compared with the value of your product to the prospect.

Don't leave your policy "for inspection." If he buys it, he can have it permanently. Be in command. His feeling of being deprived of something he wants will move him.

Remember how thousands who never manifested any interest in drinking suddenly developed an appetite for it when prohibition was enacted. It's the age-old rule: people want what they can't have.

It is often better to refuse your prospect unless he buys, than to be refused and lose the sale.

Salesmen Are Too Easily Sold

Baseball pitchers rarely make good batters. They believe in *the power of pitching* to get batters out. Similarly salesmen rarely are shrewd buyers. They are "pushovers" for other salesmen.

Don't let the prospect sell you on the idea that he will keep the merchandise to "inspect it a little while longer."

Thousands of sales are lost because salesmen went into their final drive while the prospect still had possession of the product.

If you observed my technique in an interview, you would note that I give the prospect the policy, take it back, and then go on to make my closing review of the vital issues.

Salesmen are much too anxious to please. This does not mean that you should leave your prospect with an unfriendly feeling. But too many salesmen take solace in the "if nothing else at least I left a good taste in the prospect's mouth" attitude.

The bromide that "the customer is always right" does not apply until he *becomes* a customer.

In my free energy salesmanship I am often told by prospects, "Give us a written report and we'll think it over."

It was a great day for me when I awakened to the fact that they were stalling for time, and that giving them that time was not in their best interests.

Now, my retort is, "That's a good idea, but written reports take a great deal of time. Let's put the insurance into effect immediately so that you have the benefit of protection in the meantime. After that, we can take the time to work out the details."

This plea usually closes the sale. It take courage to close at this point, but what sustains me is that I know it is in the prospect's best interest.

Salesmanship exchanges merchandise for money. Time spent on the prospect's problems is an integral part of the merchandise. If the prospect fails to buy, he is wasting a valuable portion of the merchandise. On that basis alone, the close should be made.

"No Charge or Obligation" Offers

You will encounter many prospects who completely disregard "no charge or obligation" offers.

They are simply too experienced and intelligent to bite on the something-for-nothing hook.

If, however, you ever do offer service with no strings attached, show such genuine sincerity that your prospect cannot help but accept it graciously, and without any doubts.

You can knock yourself out with free service. "We will give

you $1,000,000 of service in hopes you will spend $10 with us" is a routine I do not advocate. This type of promise is never convincing to a prospect. He's not naive; he doesn't believe it. Would you?

Goods are much harder to give away than to sell. Sell them!

Personally, I see no point in going through the rugged salesmanship required to give merchandise away. With far less effort, I can sell it, and in addition, get paid for doing so.

Our extraordinarily high standard of living is a direct result of the fact that the American likes to be sold. Moreover, he likes to *feel sold*, when he is sold. Making him feel sold is your job as a salesman. He wants you to do your work well. Do it that way and you'll win the game, which is making the sale.

Then you won't be in the position of the football team that makes the highest number of first downs but the lowest number of touchdowns. It's the final score that counts.

17

The "After" of the Interview

The Aftermath of an Interview Failure

It is difficult to write about salesmanship without also suggesting that a good performance must necessarily yield good results. Every experienced salesman knows, however, that the selling process is not that predictable.

You can give a perfect performance and still fail to close, and you can somehow fail every rule in the book and make the sale.

It is natural to hold post-mortems on your interviews, but it is almost as enervating to relive an interview as to experience it.

If you feel tired after a trying interview, refresh yourself briefly in some way. Take a short nap if it is practicable, read something relaxing, or get a cup of coffee. Do something to recharge your batteries. Your prospect deserves your maximum vigor and clear thinking.

Contrary to popular opinion, hindsight is not necessarily

better than foresight. Either can be wrong. The big winning Wow that fills you with such pride may not be the actual point that put over the sale. The "correction" you wished you could make on that error might have been more detrimental than the error itself—the cure might be possibly worse than the disease. You can do some pretty poor guessing about how you won or lost. You just cannot be sure.

If you must hold a post-mortem, do it in flashback. Run the interview back through your WHO—WHY—WHAT—WHERE—WHEN—HOW and WOW.

WHO. Did I size up the prospect properly? What was right? What was wrong? Where did I miss? What did I fail to find out?

WHY. Did I advance the best reasons why he should buy my merchandise? Did I engender in him the feeling that he was doing business with the best salesman for him?

WHAT. Did I offer the merchandise best fitted for his particular needs?

WHERE and WHEN. Did I arrange the interview in the most favorable place and time? Did I guess wrong and get a tough break?

WOW. Did I make the right "big talking point" and did I use it at the most propitious moment? Did I let him sell me his WOW of an objection? If so, how did it happen?

HOW. Did I use the appropriate sales tools (literature, etc.)? Did I exploit them fully? Did I test for a close every time I ought? What did I do wrong? What did I do right?

Conclude your post-mortems on the note: "What did I do right?" Salvage some positive things from a negative result—the things you feel convinced were right—and put them to work as soon as you can.

It's the Next Call That Counts

I used to meditate on a park bench or in my car after a difficult interview, doing my post-mortems. I would feel so demoralized, and the recovery period seemed endless.

Now, I shake off the effects of an unsuccessful interview in a matter of seconds, though this was certainly not the case when I first started.

Feelings of frustration and failure have a tendency to linger. They can be extremely agonizing. But you *can* overcome these negative feelings by setting up positive ones immediately.

Only by working out a constructive pattern of activity, in fact, can you overcome the discouraging effects of a disappointing interview. And you should establish this pattern as a definite habit. It is of infinite value in building successful salesmanship.

First, of course, do as I have already suggested in this chapter: "Salvage some positive things from a negative result—the things you feel convinced were right—and put them to work as soon as you can." Proceed to your next call fortified with the positive values you gained from the unsuccessful interview (instead of defeated by the negative results).

Treat that next call as if it were the first one of the day. Resell yourself on yourself; rekindle the flame. Then resell yourself on what you plan to do next.

The salesman's "Thanksgiving soliloquy" suggested in the third chapter of this book might have a salutary effect here. I practice it all the time. I reaffirm my appreciation for being a salesman constantly: "If I were working in an office right now, I would be drearily watching the clock, waiting for the day to end. Here I am, the master of my own destiny.

If I worked in a factory, a foreman would be looking over my shoulder, watching my every move. I would be a mechanical robot. Instead I am lucky to be a salesman."

Quite aside from post-mortems, there are sometimes hangovers from one interview to the next. Each interview is a separate entity and frequently unrelated to any other. It is treacherous to carry over any of your reactions to one prospect or interview to any other. These feelings are unfair to the next prospect and ultimately to you too.

The Successful Interview. Exploit the Elation That Follows—Drugless Euphoria

The successful interview produces a real sense of elation —of euphoria—in you. It is as though Verse 24 of Psalms 118, "This is the day which the Lord hath made; we will rejoice and be glad in it," were written for you. You feel much like the proverbial superman.

Success often begets success. While this feeling of success is still fresh, take it into the next interview.

Your sense of well-being and self-assurance can have a remarkable influence on subsequent interviews. You'll realize an unusual degree of rapport with the prospect, you are able to direct and control the course of the interview with ease, and your whole approach is fully energized. It is a kind of magical touch when properly exploited.

Now these results can be yours if (and it is a big *if*) you don't interfere with the productive exploitation of success. There are many factors which *can* interfere and are familiar to all of us.

If success creates in you feelings of self-importance, smug conceit or overconfidence, you are doomed to blunder. When you become intoxicated with an exaggerated idea of yourself and your abilities, you become insensitive to the prospect and the interview.

As you know, you cannot control all the conditions and time for opportunity in an interview. You can (and should) create the conditions that will best provide opportunities for selling, but beyond that, you must rely upon your alertness and creative imagination for exploiting every potential opportunity as it comes up. If you are carried away with your own power of success, you will be blind to these potential opportunities.

Pompous elation will give you only the sound of your own voice; unless you listen attentively to your prospect and exercise genuine concern over his needs, your sale is killed.

Overconfidence in selling, as in athletics or in politics, spells disaster. When you are too sure of your win, you aren't going to plan out or work your selling campaign carefully and thoroughly. You're going to skim over the top and put only part of your energies into your endeavor. Obviously, this can hardly produce success. You've seen it fail on many fronts.

Sometimes you emerge from a successsful interview with an overzealous attitude toward the next prospect. Usually, this pressure will simply force the prospect right out of your grasp.

Valuable By-Products of the Interview. Referred Leads and How to Handle Them

After your merchandise is delivered, your client is usually favorably disposed toward you. Your relationship with him is closer and this should be the logical time for him to do more for you. He can, too—through referred leads.

If it is a truism that "misery loves company," it might also be true that a man may feel magnanimous and altruistic about his new acquisition. He may want his friends and colleagues to enjoy similar benefits. Frequently, people are eager to share their "finds."

In suggesting leads, your client is gratifying this need and, in effect, can offer a twofold benefit. He can, in this way, contribute to the good of his friends and to the salesman as well.

Each sale is a potential lead to other sales. Word-of-mouth advertising is tremendously effective, but you, too, must take the initiative in exploiting the satisfied client for referrals.

However magnanimous your client may be, don't assume that referred leads are just handed to you. You must ferret them out from your client. You have to *sell* your client on the idea.

Here is a suggested approach:

"Since what you have bought will do so much for you and your family, who among your friends are the other up-and-coming young men, whose positions could be similarly improved?"

Here is another type of approach:

SALESMAN (*dolorously*): "The fact that I sold you cost me a great deal." (Pause.)

CLIENT (*jolted*): "What are you talking about?"

SALESMAN: "My prospects are my stock in trade, my resources. Now that you have become a client, I have lost you as a prospect. Can you suggest anyone as your successor on my list of potential prospects?"

CLIENT (*expansively*): "Well, my friend Jim Smith knows what I'm buying. He wanted to know what it was all about."

SALESMAN: "Tell me something about this Jim Smith. Is he in your social group? Is he in about the same income bracket?

The client tells you a lot about the WHO of your new prospect.

Any referred lead is also a responsibility. You cannot afford to let down the client who referred you to his successor.

Personally, I never use letters of introduction. I want to get the prospect "on my own." The card or letter of introduction too often accomplishes little more than a courteous reception and a friendly conversation about the man who referred me, *but no sales results.* I want a new client—not conversation.

Don't rush head-on to the referred prospect. He may be easily bruised. The riper he is for picking, the sweeter the fruit. Let him "mature" a while before you contact him, but not too long.

18

Goals and Growth

Sometimes I've felt that certain prospects must have been born tough. More often than not the tough prospect is the resultant product of his previous experience with salesmen.

Every salesman wants and pursues a worthwhile prospect. To me, the so-called tough prospect is one whose mind is closed, who has a "Do Not Disturb" sign hung from his neck. But for some inexplicable reason I've felt all along there was some sales promise in him. He might be short on tact and simple kindness toward salemen, but he is long on buying power. The salesman must distinguish between the market and the market place.

Penetrating the steel armor of the tough prospect has become a goal of achievement for me—part of my plan to increase my "average" sale.

For me, the realization of goals and ambitions is the mainstay of my career. From my point of view, a desirable goal has four properties:

1. It must be possible to achieve.
2. It must be a real challenge.

3. It should require time and effort, such as calls and sales per day.
4. It should be capable of growth. This means that succesive goals can be pyramided into higher and higher goals.

When I first started to sell life insurance I made fifty calls a day. My goal was simple and general: find prospects and sell them.

Then, when I progressed beyond the raw apprenticeship stage, I aimed at one $5,000 sale a day. I would start at 9:00 in the morning and keep going until 9:00 at night if necessary. Rarely did I fail to achieve my goal. On the basis of 300 selling days a year, $5,000 a day produces an annual sales volume of $1,500,000. When I was reaching that mark consistently, I saw the vistas of a higher plateau, serener and greener, already reached by other salesmen.

From this point on, I really enjoyed selling. Instead of a mere job, I considered it a contest, and each prospect became a playing partner.

Now I had to study the ratio of calls to interviews, and the ratio of interviews to sales. Fifty calls, ten interviews, one sale, was my first attained goal. But with free energy salesmanship, I upgraded to one sale for every five interviews, and then one sale for every three interviews. My sales continued to increase to over $3,000,000 a year.

To produce greater results for each sale, I had to seek out tougher prospects. To sell them, I had to use much more resourcefulness in practicing the principles of free energy salesmanship.

I succeeded in selling many difficult prospects. This resulted in larger sales for each call.

The daily sales constituted my bread-and-butter earnings; the tough ones were the cake with frosting on it.

I soon discovered that the tough prospects taught me a great deal in the art of selling, and dealing with them profitably became part of my regular routine. As a result, there were no really tough prospects.

Quotas to me are simply unrealized goals. In planning for growth, I always try to establish primary and secondary plateaus without worrying about the more rarefied air at the higher levels.

It's easier and takes less strain to look down rather than up. But looking down merely shows where you have been. That is "history"; but there is also tomorrow and the future. That requires looking up and ahead.

Apart from any theological theories, my personal concept of sin and of the fallen angel is that of falling below the level of one's capabilities.

My ego is tied in with my work—that of a salesman with high standards. I suffer severely if I fail to measure up to my ego concept.

Mealtime for Action-Time Means Sales

Never lunch alone if you can lunch with a prospect. Meet prospects for breakfast, for coffee, and, of course, for dinner. Convert mealtimes into dollars.

Getting the prospect to share a meal with you is a sale in itself in your "one-plus-one-equals-one" sequence.

Here is how I handled one prospect in trying to arrange a lunch appointment. Originally, the prospect had replied to a direct-mail piece. I phoned him.

PROSPECT: "I like your ideas and would like to read more about them. But please just mail me your booklet. I am not ready to talk to you."

My reply: "I would like to meet you because I have some new ideas *which are not in the booklet* or any of the other published material. When will you be free for lunch? I could join you when you take a coffee break? How about breakfast together some morning?"

This is my "mealtime for action-time" sales technique.

The main object of the joint meal should be the WHO of the prospect. Never, if you can help it, discuss the prospect's situation in the presence of a third party. Never expose a prospect's affairs to any chance of gossip. Even when the prospect insists upon talking business while others are present, stop him if you consider it unwise. You must protect your prospect even when he does not protect himself.

Sometimes it is preferable to eliminate business conversations from mealtime appointments. There are no absolutes in free energy salesmanship.

This is what occurred in another situation.

PROSPECT: "My office is a pretty crowded place for this discussion."

My reply: "Come on. Get your hat and let's go out for a cup of coffee at some place where we can talk without interruption."

"Sweat Questions" Can Get a Prospect to Join You at a Meal

In order to put the prospect in the right frame of mind, I use these questions; they are designed to arouse interest and make the prospect want to meet me:

"Are there any stepchildren in your family?"

"Are you disinheriting some of your children?"

"Is your wife's side of the family ending up with all of your money?"

"Are your insurance policies equipped with all the free extras?"

"Do you have the free benefits to which you are entitled,

such as spendthrift provisions, common disaster clauses, lapse-proof provision, etc., in your life insurance policies?"

"Will 180 million strangers share your money when you die?"

"What have you done about taking the inflation out of your life insurance?"

"Do you know about your sizable bank account in Baltimore?" (Social Security)

"Are you paying an insurance company to protect you, and then letting it off the hook?"

"Are you familiar with Uncle Sam's bequest for you and your family?"

"Is your life insurance going to hurt your children's ambitions?"

I know men who will scream that such questions are poor public relations for the insurance business because they suggest possible weaknesses in the service. However, the principles of free energy salesmanship declare that if you can't create in the prospect some awareness of his problems, you will not imbue him with the drive to buy.

Never offer the answers to the above questions on the phone. Use these questions whenever possible, to bring about a personal meeting. Explaining the answers is precisely the reason you and the prospect should meet for lunch. After lunch, sell him, or to reverse this method, you might have the interview before lunch, explaining your answers and selling your product first.

Indeed I seldom have to go through the foregoing roster of questions completely.

The moment the prospect asks me to elaborate or explain a particular question more fully, I make my move to suggest a joint meeting with him.

Let me quote what I then reply to him:

"The very fact that this is still unclear to you is more reason why you will benefit from our meeting together."

Usually the prospect's objection to such a meeting is his lack of time. Anticipating this, I add: "Both you and I have to eat, so why not have lunch together?"

You Must Be Willing to Advance. Sink or Swim

There is an old saying to the effect that quicksand is like thin ice; you can stay on top, provided you keep moving, but if you stand still, you will sink.

You must continue to raise your sights, and as you do, you also raise those of your costumers, and they grow with you. Then, you'll find that you sell more with no added effort.

When my General Agent, "Coop" Curry, tells me it is time to raise my sights, I accept his judgment. He is always right. I know salesmen who resist that idea, but a good sales manager, like a good second in the ring, knows better than you what you are able to do.

Here is an appropriate place to express my warm gratitude for the stimulus given me by "Coop" Curry in extending my horizons. Mr. Curry is a matchless builder of men, and inspiring them to ascend to greater heights is an important part of such construction. I consider myself fortunate to have begun my apprenticeship in his shop.

When your sights go up, and your goals are expanded, some aspects of your selling become easier. The best qualified prospect is a more willing listener. It is easier to talk to him if you have studied him and determined how your merchandise can best serve his needs, the role that it can assume in his over-all financial situation. He may not be the easiest man to close, but when you do close, you and he are substantially ahead.

I never change anything that is working for me. I keep it working and add something else. To add more, I must learn more.

Exploit Every Opportunity

Opportunity is considerate. It makes few appointments, but it is more likely to knock if you are at home.

I was aboard a plane flying to a convention in Florida. With me were five other life insurance salesmen. Each of us had sold over $1,000,000 in life insurance during the year. Suddenly the plane was forced to make an emergency landing on a farm. I realized that then, if ever, men would be more sharply aware that death is always at their elbows. I sold life insurance to both pilots, the stewardess and two passengers. The other insurance men did no more than moan with the other passengers.

Very often, I commute by train from my home to my office, a distance of twenty-seven miles. I usually engage my seat companion in conversation. I try to channel the subject to his financial affairs, if possible. Quite often it turns out that he needs life insurance for the protection of his family.

To me, opportunity means any chance to offer the use of my merchandise for the best interests of the other fellow. That is my attitude. I can't emphasize enough that in free energy salesmanship, *attitude is far more important than aptitude.*

Also, opportunity, to me, means constant self-examination and development, by learning to do better what I have been doing all along.

PART II

The Journeyman
Stage Two

19

The Second Stride— The Journeyman Stage

How You Recognize That You Have Reached There

Malcolm Adam, president of Penn Mutual Life Insurance Company, tapped me on the shoulder one day.

"Karl," he said, "never before has a Penn Mutual Agent sold three million of life insurance in a single year. I think you're ripe now and the very man who can do it."

It was a challenge, an astonishing one. I don't suppose that *any* salesman who is on his way up realizes how carefully he is being watched.

I accepted Malcolm Adam's challenge—but where to begin? I couldn't reach that $3 million mark by making more calls a day. Already, I was making as high as seventy calls a day, counting the phone solicitations and personal interviews.

I never have believed that Malcolm Adam cared too much

about the $3 million volume as such. He challenged me for quite another reason. He wanted me to take inventory of myself.

Mr. Adam's judgment was correct. I broke that $3 million mark. I did it that very year.

It was in May, at a convention, that Malcolm Adam challenged me. There were seven months remaining in that year. I had done a little over $1 million during the first five months, an average of $200,000 a month. I needed a fifty per cent increase, a step-up to $300,000 a month, almost on the nose, for each of those seven months.

Without accelerating my pace, I took the stride. I maintained that pace for another year. Later, I stepped it up some more and lengthened the stride.

It might be interesting to consider how such a remarkable increase in production came about in a relatively short period.

A good part of the explanation lies in the fact that I started to dig the old field more deeply and intensively. Instead of spreading my energies thin in search of more and more prospects, I recognized that it would greatly conserve my time if I went over the cultivated territory—my clients—and planted a new crop for them in the form of life insurance.

Then, too, I exploited every opportunity to adjust and convert into permanent insurance any temporary or term insurance in the portfolios of my clients.

To my own amazement, from the moment I reached the higher plateau of production, I never regressed. The momentum of free energy salesmanship kept me going full steam ahead.

It should be evident that this surge in production was accomplished by retooling for greater effectiveness and efficiency, in the same way that a factory must do in order to function at maximum production.

The Transition

In free energy salesmanship, the transition from apprentice to journeyman is not abrupt.

The time required to master each level varies with each salesman. There is no arbitrary time-requirement, such as two years or four years of apprenticeship selling, before you qualify for the journeyman stage. There are no attendant ceremonies to acknowledge your "graduation" from the first level (although one day some smart sales managers will accord it some ritualistic observance.)

You just realize one day that you have experienced hundreds and hundreds of interviews, using the WHO—WHY—WHAT—WHERE—WHEN—WOW—HOW technique, and that you now know exactly what will work for you in handling a prospect.

I considered myself a journeyman when (a) I had acquired enough experience and know-how with my product to be at ease and self-assured in my presentations to the general run of prospects, (b) I no longer had to consult my superiors frequently or send for help when trying to resolve tough problems with my merchandise, (c) I had worked out enough selling methods that "produced," and (d) I had worked with the "one-plus-one-equals-one" process until I could trust it to produce a higher than average number of sales per one hundred interviews.

At that point, I did some self-appraising.

As a journeyman, I continued to stay with my regular clients and grow with them. I sold no more policies than I did as an apprentice, but I found the average client much easier to sell; moreover, the average-size policy was considerably larger—it was as simple as that.

When I reached the journeyman stage, I pursued the tough prospects—the ones with the financial ability to buy bigger policies. At the same time I upgraded my "little" clients, those of modest means whose original policies dated back to my days as an apprentice.

As a Journeyman Your Time Is Money

As you evolve into a free energy salesman, your value increases. You've improved your uses of sales tools, to be sure, but beyond that, you have learned the art of using your time to best advantage.

You are the management in control of your time. A sales manager may tell you how many calls to make, but only you can control the time involved in preparing and planning the interviews. That is the time that counts most.

Figure it out in dollars and cents.

During the typical business day, when a colleague invites me out for a cup of coffee, I say, "I would rather give you a dollar and let you have your coffee without me."

To me, time is worth several hundred dollars a day. Thirty minutes spent over a friendly cup of coffee with anyone who is not a prospect could, conceivably, cost me a great deal of money in earnings.

I use the telephone. The value of a three-minute call is, to me, $5.00. Of this, the telephone company gets only a dime.

Before going out on an appointment, I always confirm it by phone. I can't afford to waste ten minutes waiting, if, by a phone call, I can cut it down to three minutes or less.

The More Valuable Your Hours, the More Important the Minutes

Every journeyman should have a general work plan for his business days. A few special days require special plans.

As a rule, I spend my mornings, while other men are busiest with details, on (*a*) my personal affairs and (*b*) setting up a date for luncheon with a prospect.

Those lunch-time minutes are likely to be the only ones that my biggest prospects and clients can give me. Those particular minutes have to pay me far more than my average value per minute. I will spend an hour, even two hours if necessary, getting the right kind of luncheon appointment. Usually, however, it requires much less time than that. When the appointment is arranged, I am relaxed to handle details and phone calls from clients.

The details I have referred to above include a painstaking, systematic analysis of my clients' records. I explore in detail any possible chance to be of service. Always allow time for policy service details. Rarely do I overlook the needs of a client, but when I have done so, a competitor has gotten in and plugged the gap. Fortunately, that seldom happens. The most fruitful use you can put your time to is servicing the insurance needs of your clients.

Years ago, during my apprenticeship days, I devoted my morning hours to sales calls. At that time, that pattern fitted in best with my work plan. Now, although my daily activities are much different, the fact is that I am, in the last analysis, still an apprentice.

I still strive to study and learn new ideas and techniques the way an apprentice must. I still make calls en route home, *if I have failed to make my sale for the day.* I insist on making a minimum of one sale each business day. I've never changed this primary goal: a sale a day keeps my creditors away.

Nor have I divorced myself from any of the fundamental objectives and goals so intimately associated with my years as an apprentice. Some that I still continue to practice diligently are:

(*a*) To arrange or confirm a luncheon appointment with a prospect for this day, or some other time in the future.

(*b*) To make at least one sale during such a luncheon appointment. I should either complete a sale of a policy, or at least set up an appointment for a medical examination. This is the gateway to a sale.

(*c*) To arrange for delivery of policies, by appointment, to avoid mislaying them or cluttering up my office. The appointment will save you the possibility of a long trip to the client's office for nothing.

(*d*) To ask of every client the name of a potential prospect so as to keep building new links to my ever-growing chain of clients.

(*e*) To utilize to the maximum, the special abilities and training of other men in auxiliary specialized fields, in order that my clients may have the best available guidance and service.

(*f*) To keep abreast of all major innovations and services as they develop in my industry and my particular product. In this way, my clients are afforded the benefit of vital information pertaining to the rules as well as the exceptions, as it is released.

(*g*) To plow back some of my earnings into improving my facilities in order to offer ever more complete service to my clients.

(*h*) To keep my "light" burning with my clients. Out of

sight—out of mind, and the loss can prove very costly. I must, in some way, keep my name before my clients all the time.

(*i*) To make a practice of helping my fellow salesmen, in appreciation for what I always learn from them.

No salesman should delude himself into thinking that he can graduate from the apprentice stage permanently by rejecting the goals and objectives related to that period of his development. They are fundamental and the basis for all effective salesmanship.

20

A Collection of
Miscellaneous Ideas

How I Regard My Business

In many ways, my position is analogous to that of a store-keeper. I must maintain regular hours (minimum) like a store. During store hours, someone must mind the business. I am that someone.

All the time I am not working during those store hours, I am in a store that is virtually closed for business.

If I don't think and plan out my calls, then I am inviting my customers into an unstocked or, at least, poorly stocked store.

When I don't arrange to see a prospect during lunch, I am hanging an "out to lunch" sign on my door.

If I waste time on personal calls that could be accomplished just as well by phone, then other prospects who could be reached never get to my store at all.

The best "deal" for my prospect always turns out to be the best one for me.

If I am worried about personal or business problems, I am

136

precluding business. Worry will always interfere with the ability to do work effectively—the value of my work becomes proportionately less. My work in salesmanship is part of the merchandise in my store. To reduce the value of that merchandise is to also reduce the amount of business my store will do.

I will conduct the business of my store in such a way that worry and anxiety can least affect me.

Thinking in terms of the best interests of my prospect is the most effective way to keep my worries at a minimum.

The Client's Bill of Rights

Every client is entitled to life, liberty and the pursuit of his own best interest.

The client's best interest shall be paramount. When a salesman's business practices fail to reflect the best interests of the prospect, the prospect has the right to eliminate the salesman.

The client's freedom of speech during the interview shall not be abridged.

He shall not be denied his right to be sold on what he buys.

All clients and all prospects are created free and equal, regardless of their respective financial status.

Each client and prospect has the full right to as much of the salesman's service time as is required.

The salesman shall practice no interview techniques that handicap the interview with any consideration of the customer's race, creed, politics, sports opinions, or anything else extraneous to the function of selling the client.

It is the client's inalienable right to demand that every sales interview be carefully planned and be an interesting and profitable experience.

All the foregoing rights of the client shall be recognized as conservers of the time and multipliers of the profit of the salesman.

Tough Prospects Can Be Tenderized by the Journeyman

Goats can be as stubborn as mules. Never meet a goat head-on or steal up behind a mule.

When I know that I am coming up against a prospect who is tough to sell, I try to find out whether he is the kind who loves to bully a salesman, or is the type who is poised until he gets ahead of you and then kicks your sales idea to pieces.

All that is part of the WHO in the preparation for the interview. As a rule, the tough man has defeated enough salesmen, and may have even boasted of it to enough of his friends, that this side of him is quite generally known.

For the "sock it to him" prospect, I try to have something new to offer. While he is "frothing at the mouth," he usually reveals enough about why he will *not* buy the particular merchandise I am offering to indicate what he *is* willing to buy.

The tougher a prospect is, the easier he will be to convert into a client, providing I can make that first sale to him. He was too tough for my competitors and he will be even tougher for them after I sell him.

Your Tongue's Revolutions-Per-Minute (RPM's)

Rightly, you might wonder why any space is devoted here to a consideration of the pace or speed of the salesman's presentation to the prospect.

You might even conclude, unfortunately, from the observations following that a fast-talking salesman can outwit his prospect with a gushing "pitch."

The only purpose of this material is to emphasize the vital importance of adjusting the salesman's pace to the prospect's capacity to hear and absorb, and possibly even "digest" the stream of words representing the ideas advanced by the salesman.

Certain foods require more chewing than others. Similarly, certain prospects require longer to assimilate the food for thought served to them by the salesman.

You must pace your gait if you want to win the race.

Some of my "better tools for better salesmanship" are devices I did not know I had until an observer of my methods told me about them. The same could be true of you, if you were so observed. We all do well some things that we are not conscious of doing at all. When we are made aware of them, and study them out, we can make them work even better. Speech pace is one of them.

The Fifteen-Second Time Limit

There is a limit to the time a salesman can "keep possession of that ball" before the prospect yells "foul." The yelling isn't audible, generally, but is an unexpressed feeling of burden, boredom and exasperation on the part of the prospect. This does not contribute to the interview. The maximum time limit seems to be about fifteen seconds. That I have learned by instinct and experience.

You can crowd all the words you are able to speak into those fifteen seconds, but after that point, you must pause. It is the prospect's turn to respond in some way: to let your words "sink in," to indicate that he wants you to continue, or do some talking himself.

The break may be made before the fifteen-second interval. I was timed by a stop watch, without my knowledge, when I said, "I've just heard about it and I don't know much about it."

The stop watch indicated that I spoke these twelve words in two seconds. That is at the rate of 360 words a minute. (A good stenographer is expected to take more than 100 words a minute.) I have been timed speaking 90 words in fifteen seconds. That again is at the rate of 360 words a minute. But I do not speak that number in a single minute.

High-speed speech is high-energy speech. It can energize the prospect, but it can also enervate him. The pauses rest him.

Rapid speech requires practice. Don't sacrifice either clarity of enunciation or good dramatic change of tone, pitch and emphasis, for the sake of speed.

Talk rapidly until you reach the big point. Then, lean forward a little, slow down (my speech pace goes down to about twenty-five words in fifteen seconds) and speak in a firm, confident tone.

Power Expressions for High-Speed Speech

With a rapidly spoken power expression, you can "set the prospect up"—or predispose him—for the point you want to make. Here are a few such expressions:

"This will surprise you."

"Here is something new."

"I've found a way to do you a favor."

"Here is my suggestion—what I recommend."

"Here is how you can save some money."

"This opportunity to save and make money wasn't available a year ago."

"If you wait even one week to act on this, it will cost you money."

Here is how it works out in speech pace.

SALESMAN (*rapidly*): "This will surprise you!" (*Pause, then speak slowly.*) "Here is how it will work out."

It is much like the pitcher throwing two fast balls to set the batter up for that slow curve he will hit into the double play.

Speech Cripplers and How They Spoil an Interview

If you are subject to such "speech defects" as *er* and *ah*, then you can accelerate your speech pace considerably by just eliminating them.

One of the functions (conscious or unconscious) of these devices is to "hold the air" and forestall interruption, while you organize your thinking for the rest of your sentence.

In free energy salesmanship, you want the active participation of your prospect in the interview. Never say, "I have —er—something that—ah—might surprise you."

This will not only annoy your prospect, but reduce the effectiveness of your statement. It weakens the punch.

The "er, ah, eh" business is, of course, a nervous habit. Most nervous habits handicap a sales interview, and are like little bugs which can do great damage.

21

Telephone Salesmanship

The use of the telephone as a tool in effective salesmanship is extremely important.

This medium can be used to great advantage in selling if properly employed; if it is abused, it produces nothing but an unfavorable impression.

Telephoning is such a familiar means of communication, it might seem superfluous to go into the simple mechanics of it. However, through such regular and frequent use, we unwittingly fall into poor habits at times. These poor habits may have little consequence in social communication (and then again, may not), but when practiced in telephone salesmanship they can be a serious detriment to selling or good business relations.

For best results, speak directly into the mouthpiece and keep it about one half-inch away. Use a normal speaking voice. Shouting is shattering to your listener and unintelligible as well. The inaudible voice is equally annoying and ineffective.

If your office or room is noisy when you call, you can relieve much of the disturbance of that noise by covering the mouthpiece with your hand when you are not speaking.

There are a number of books available strictly devoted to the art of telephone selling. Many are valuable aids in this whole technique, and I suggest you check your library or technical book sources for this material.

How to Make the Most of Your Telephone Techniques

As with your personal interview methods, you must analyze and evaluate your telephone techniques. Keep tab on the various approaches that work favorably for you and incorporate them into your regular telephone techniques. On the other hand, those which seem to interfere with productive telephone selling should be eliminated.

Here are some points that I find help me in my telephone salesmanship:

(1) Whether you are meeting your prospect face-to-face or are talking to him on the telephone, you use the same WHO—WHY—WHAT—WHERE—WHEN—WOW—HOW process that is the basic structure of the interview. After sufficient experience, as a journeyman, this process requires a minimum of time.

A poorly organized call made to the right place (such as the man's home rather than his office) and at the right time, can produce better results than the strongest telephone sales talk made to the wrong place and at the wrong time.

(2) Make a point of pronouncing the name of your prospect correctly at the outset, and again throughout the interview. Every man is energized by the sound of his own name, correctly pronounced.

(3) Always answer the phone with warm cordiality. This invites a sympathetic response.

The common practice of answering in a cold, apprehensive manner, and then warming up when you discover it is a client, is objectionable to me. My friendliness is unconditional and for all, for I believe that the first impression in a call is particularly important. This even applies to calls from people I know well. If the first impression indicates suspicion on my part, the subsequent discovery that the party calling is someone I want to please comes too late to mend the situation.

(4) When I initiate a call to a man I do not know and find him out, I do not leave my number for call back. I call him again; thus I preclude his return call from reaching me at some inopportune time. I can control the time and conditions of my contact much better this way.

(5) If my secretary has promised that I will call back, I do so. I feel a verbal commitment is a contract you must not fail.

(6) I follow the formula: one hour of work by telephone is equal to one day of making personal calls, whether driving or on foot. Nonetheless, I seek every good means to conserve my telephone time.

(7) When I reach my prospect, I first pronounce his name, then announce my own, and finally open with a terse power expression such as "I have something new for you."

His voice and manner in reply tell me almost everything I need to know about his reaction. This is the barometer for my next statement.

(8) I frequently use abbreviated questions, such as: "Your name? Married or single? Age? Income? Approximately, of course."

If the prospect is somewhat evasive about income, avoid a long or apologetic explanation.

The fast action is energizing to the interview, and I maintain the spirit of energizing the prospect. His hesitation is a caution signal to me. I can then adjust my own action accordingly.

(9) In my experience, high-speed speech is even more effective on the phone than in personal interviews. Change of pace can produce the same effect. If I were a naturally slow speaker, I probably would find that the slow speech technique worked well for me on the phone. My phone calls are timed at exactly the same speed as my personal interviews, ninety words per fifteen seconds.

(10) The well-modulated voice and the use of pauses are just as important on the telephone as in face-to-face contacts.

(11) Often a phone call conveys a sense of urgency. Many men who will not stop for anything else will answer their telephones. Keep the salesmanship energy flowing and that sense of urgency can generate action. If you want quick action, use the telephone!

(12) Just as I conserve time for selling by having other people take care of personal matters for me whenever feasible, I economize on time further by never using personal interview time for a salesmanship job that can be accomplished as well by phone.

(13) Above all, always keep *your objective* in mind. In my case, I am either selling an appointment, or a medical examination to qualify my prospect, in order to open the door for a subsequent appointment.

22

The Journeyman Stage and Related Aspects

The Journeyman and the Theater of the Interview

A story is told about the famous John Barrymore. On one occasion while the actor was out in the rural areas working on location, he lost a personal wager. As a consequence, he had to go on stage in an amateur production in the local firehouse. The time was immediately—no rehearsals. His name was unannounced and he played anonymously. He was simply given permission by the manager of the show and walked onto a stage that was completely alien to him.

He was dressed in ordinary street clothes and the stage was almost bare of props. He reached for a vase and it became a sword. At first, the audience giggled, but soon they were thrilled as never before by the performance. A master was at work. The theater was wherever he was, and the settings and props were whatever he found at hand.

I am certainly no Barrymore, but in my selling career I

have been known to drive a prospect into the city, and failing to find a parking space, continued to drive around the streets until I made my sale.

In his own best interest, the prospect needed to be insured against hazards and catastrophe. I needed a common denominator between him and me. It was the problem of finding parking space. He was annoyed, but the hazards against which he needed protection could be far more significant than mere annoyance. There was the sale, and of such stuff sales are made.

How to Resolve Some Important "If's"

If you meet a potential prospect in a social situation or any other place where it is inappropriate to discuss business, *don't talk business.* Do "put a bug in his ear." Provoke his interest and intrigue him with a statement like, "the men in this crowd could save a million dollars a year on their income taxes." Then, casually walk away.

If you are planting an idea in a prospect's mind, don't linger and "read" his face to see how he responds. You'll be trapped and waste the opportunity. Wait and get in touch with him a day or so later, or even a week later. Then you can set your stage and hold your interview.

If, while you are on a commute train, you can meet men who can contribute to your business, don't withdraw and read during the trip. Talk with them; exploit the opportunity.

If men who can help you wish to drive you to work, don't insist on driving your own car. Ride with them and pay their parking fees—just as you would do for your own car.

If you can phone, don't write. A phone call is faster, good economy, and more flexible. Moreover, you don't have to wait and hope for an answer.

If a phone call fails to do the job, but a letter will, don't hold a personal interview—write. Always conserve your salesmanship hours in every way.

If you are not completely broke, don't type your own letters. Stenographic service costs are nominal and they free your energy and time for selling. What's more, you get a better job.

If you can afford your own dictating, adding, or other business machine, don't "hold out" for the boss to buy them for you. While you are waiting, you are losing the valuable use and advantage of them. This represents poor business economy.

If you can get a good slogan, don't treat it as a meaningless quip to embellish your stationery. Live up to its meaning in your business practice.

Mine, you will remember, is "I don't sell insurance. I help you buy it."

How to Verify an Appointment

Before leaving for an appointment, I always verify it by phone first. In this way, I don't waste time waiting after I arrive for the interview.

I am likely to do a bit of pre-selling and even some stage-setting in this pre-interview phone call.

"Good morning, Mr. Edwards." (*Pause.*) "I am on my way to your office for our ten o'clock appointment. You are going to hear something new and surprising about the savings you can make on taxes."

It is by no means an exception to make the sale right there and then by phone, and never have to keep the interview appointment. That is not the point of the call. However, your attitude should always be flexible enough to handle any eventuality, and particularly a quick sale.

If you should be delayed, then don't just proceed to the appointment. Phone ahead and tell him when you can arrive. Don't offer a series of excuses; they waste time. Your arrival time is the primary issue.

Some sage has said, "Punctuality is the thief of time." No one wants to be punctual and then have to wait. Don't expect the other man to be punctual and then make him wait. Many of my appointments today are made not for some arbitrary hour like 10:30, but rather between 10:30 and 11:00. That system deprives punctuality of its time-thieving nature. Phone ahead and say, "Now we can be definite. I find that 10:45 is more convenient for me, but I'll be glad to make it 10:30 if that suits you better."

You must be specific to be in command. Maintaining command of the interview is fundamental to free energy salesmanship.

How to Trigger Action

One of the most effective devices for inciting action from an indecisive prospect is by the use of a "shocker." It often acts like a catalyst on the passive prospect who just won't act.

I use "shockers" freely; however, they must be true and not contrived. Unless the shocker is an actual experience, it does not convince the prospect of either its truth or its merit.

To one man I said, "This man died before we could put his $50,000 policy into force."

To another, "He paid $20,000 more in income taxes than he should have paid, last year."

I also include some of the details relating to a recent case demonstrating my point. Often I substantiate my statements with real documents, news clippings, photostats of death claim, check payments, etc.

This type of technique will emphasize, too, that you know your business and product well.

Energize your interview. Use your shocker only where a jolt will work. Mean what you say and be sure of the facts.

Interviews in Technicolor

The ball-point pen or other gift I use as a business card establishes the feeling, "I am here to give you something you want."

Color can influence feeling or mood.

On one occasion, I had to offer an alternate proposition to a prospect. Trying to grasp both propositions at the same time became a problem to him.

As an aid in clarifying the plans to my prospect, I used a red ink pen for outlining one proposition, and a blue one for the other plan.

He got the idea quickly. Soon he was talking about the "red" deal and the "blue" deal. By identifying each plan with a simple symbol like color, he was no longer confused.

He decided on the "blue" deal. He wanted stability in his affairs, and blue, so the color experts say, helps convey the feeling of comfort and stability. Red gives the feeling of action, unless a man has the "stop-on-red and go-on-green" pattern of thinking.

Suspense as a Sales Teaser

One of my tough prospects kept me on the hook for months, promising that he would call me when he was ready, and he took his own good time about it.

To accelerate some action from him, I called, suggesting that he submit to a medical examination. It should be self-evident by now that selling the idea of a medical examination is my standard door-and-mind opener.

When I proposed this, he offered the common reply: "I don't see any sense in my taking a medical exam."

"Are you afraid you might not qualify?" I challenged.

He finally acquiesced, "All right. I'll take the exam, but I won't buy insurance."

I made no further comment, but arranged for the appointment.

About two weeks later, he phoned to check on the results of the examination.

"I haven't yet heard from the company," I said. I actually hadn't, of course; however I was pleased for this opportunity to keep him in suspense.

In a day or two I did receive the information on his examination, and he did qualify. I did not advise my prospect, however. I decided that it would be better strategy to hold out for a bit.

The following week, he phoned me again. This time he could not conceal his anxiety. "What's holding up that policy? Is anything wrong?"

I knew intuitively that this was the propitious moment. Happily I responded, "I am delighted to tell you that you passed 100 per cent. Now, let's get together."

From that time on, he has been a valued client of mine.

The principle involved here is that after I got him in motion, I held out until his anxiety energized him enough to act.

This type of strategy has made many sales for me.

An Apparently Exhausted Mine and a New Vein of Gold, or Creative Imagination Produces Sales

The prospect, a distinguished lawyer in my area, accepted my ball-point pen calling card with complete, but courteous, indifference. He listened with formal restraint. Clearly, no prospect was less salable.

He said, "One of the other top agents just called on me, but there is no reason for me to buy insurance."

I did some more probing into the WHO of my prospect. I learned that he had been widowed and had no children. His wife was a victim of cancer, and he was devoted to helping cancer research. He had never remarried.

The WHY and WHAT required much more study. I doubt if the other salesman recognized the need for stimulating the prospect's interest in cancer research.

Using this information about his interest in cancer research as a clue, I had to design a plan that would satisfy that interest.

He purchased a large policy which, upon his death, will bequeath a considerable grant to cancer research.

Personally, I was thrilled with my role in helping him establish a charitable foundation in his wife's memory.

He, the lawyer, handled all the legal aspects, and in that way could participate actively in the transaction.

Due to his wife's death, as a taxpayer with no dependents, his income tax bracket had risen considerably. I learned that he was particularly attached to a niece and nephew.

On this basis, I suggested that he establish trusts for these children. This, of course, resulted in more business.

He had, before the advent of my call, owned a substantial amount of life insurance. I made the necessary beneficiary changes in these policies.

Don't Just Sell—Help Your Prospect Buy

I remember when I made one of the most significant decisions in my selling career.

On one of the rare occasions when a client approached me about insurance, he announced: "I want $5,000 coverage on myself and $1,000 each on my wife and kids."

I replied, "Life insurance was designed to enable a father to protect his children, not vice versa." Then I added, "Put it all on yourself until your family is fully protected. After that, your wife and children can be covered. Women and children first. You see, I am in the lifeboat business. Later on there'll be a seat for father."

As an apprentice, I would have been so eager for the sale that I would have taken the order on the prospect's terms.

But this time I had the advantage of professional maturity. I knew the prospect was misguided in his thinking, and someone must set him straight. I was qualified to do it; moreover, it was my responsibility to act in his best interests.

My analysis of his needs and my professional recommendations had to take precedence over the sale he offered. I had to make a decision: should I take the chance of losing the man's business to some apprentice who might indiscriminately sell him on his terms, or insist on offering the plan which will best serve his interests? I was determined to orient this prospect properly on the function of insurance and the type of plan best suited for his needs. If he remained adamant about his original idea and rejected my plan, I was satisfied to lose the sale.

I am pleased to say that I was able to prevail upon him and he has developed into one of my most valued clients.

PART III
The Advanced Salesman
Stage Three

Taking The Third Stride

23

Of Things
Remembered

In this chapter, I shall attempt to depict a typical day drawn from my actual experience in each of the three stages of development in my selling career: (1) apprentice (2) journeyman (3) advanced.

As you will recognize, there is no arbitrary line of demarcation which separates one stage from the next. There is, rather, a good deal of overlapping so that many characteristics and practices of the most elementary stage are still an integral part of the experience of the advanced salesman.

My purpose in presenting this material to you is not only to help you gain information that will advance your selling career, but also to encourage and inspire you to forge ahead. Every experience, every episode, I have lived.

The rewards are many and truly gratifying.

Join Me in the Course of One Day as an Apprentice

Get up early. While still at home, search through the newspapers. Examine the Vital Statistics and Business Section for marriage announcements, birth notices, business personnel changes—in fact, anything that offers the names and addresses of people and their affairs. When the affairs of people change, their needs for life insurance change as well. Immediately, they become potential prospects.

I followed this process yesterday, too. I have accrued a long list of names. Now, it is time to make a selection and determine my schedule for the day.

As a former Fuller Brush man, I am thoroughly familiar with the city. If I were not, however, my next step would be to consult the city directory and spot all of the names on a street map. I must build my call route for the day so that my calls are efficiently consolidated. I do not want to do any backtracking if possible.

I shall go to my office. I would not go in if I didn't have something definite to do there, but this is one of the days I must learn more about my merchandise.

I have much to learn. The only sales talk I know is the one on retirement income.

It seems so simple to sell a man something he will get while he is still alive, instead of making sacrifices while he is alive to benefit others after he dies.

I have made some sales in life insurance, but I am a long way from high-level free energy salesmanship.

Since I am due at the office at 11:00 for a sales meeting, I can start making calls at 9:00. In two hours I can make twelve calls, unless I run into a hot prospect. If I should, I'll stick right with him and try to sell, of course.

I will use the only sales talk I know and embellish on it as best I can.

I plan my twelve calls along a route that begins close to my home and ends in the area of my office. These calls produce little except for a few that offered the vague hope of "see my husband tonight." It is not quite 11:00, so I have some time to use before the meeting.

This time is used for making cold-canvass calls at downtown stores, and I talk to the clerks, chiefly. I am much too afraid of "big" business men. In fact, I am afraid of so many things!

The sales meeting concluded about 2:00.

My appointment book shows that I am to deliver a policy to a recently widowed woman.

And this takes us back to a much earlier date that I want to tell you about.

Quite some time ago, I sold a policy to a small shopkeeper. For some reason, his quarterly premiums were always delayed. I always found it necessary to call at his place of business, finally, to pick up his premium check.

Collections were not part of my job, but I worried about his tendency to be delinquent since if he defaulted, his protection might be seriously jeopardized. Since he was my client, I felt obliged to give him that service.

One Friday afternoon, I realized he had failed to pay his last quarterly premium and that I could not collect it from him in due time. I decided to protect him, therefore, and advance his premium out of my own pocket. I felt sure he would reimburse me the following Monday.

On Sunday, however, he was killed in a traffic accident.

When I telephoned his widow, she said, "Don't play jokes on me. The policy lapsed."

On Tuesday, her lawyer phoned me. "Why do you insist on taunting this distressed woman? That policy lapsed and you know it."

I brought the proof of my payment to the lawyer. It confirmed that I had kept the policy in force, and it was in the amount of $50,000. What a tremendous windfall to a widow with five dependent children!

My advance was repaid, of course. The lawyer was so impressed with my loyalty that he exacted a promise from the woman to buy a policy from me to demonstrate her gratitude. The policy was to be taken on her for the protection of her young children.

It is this policy that I plan to deliver after the sales meeting. I am feeling quite confident and benevolent when I greet the woman. She, however, responds with complete disregard for what has transpired.

She announces coldly, "If I do buy life insurance, I decided to buy it from my neighbor who sells insurance."

This is a truly bitter moment! I am completely crushed and I resolve that never again will I play the fall guy or believe in the good of people. They are really a bunch of ingrates!

Well, this moment is serving its purpose, for I am able to release a good deal of my hostility by adopting such a cynical attitude. Fortunately, cynicism is contrary to my basic nature and I just can't live with this kind of thinking or feeling for very long.

Now I can look at this incident with perspective. I am sure it represents the exception and not the rule. I shall go right on trusting and believing.

At this point, I am passing a milestone in my free energy salesmanship growth, but I cannot recognize it yet.

My calls en route home are plotted along a route that closely parallels my morning route. There is a practical reason for this. If I get more "see my husband tonight" responses, I want those husbands to be living near each other.

My first call after dinner that evening is on Mr. Putnam

who lives on Seventh Avenue. He is receptive. As I begin to fill out an application, he says, "You are writing 'Putnam.' "

I looked at him quizzically.

He went on, "My name is 'Brown.' "

I discover that I am at the correct house-number, but on the wrong street. Mr. Brown lives on Sixth Avenue, but I succeed in making the sale.

The Mr. Putnam of Seventh Avenue, whom I call on later, turns out to be "no sale."

I have always been lucky, even in some of my mistakes.

In the Course of One Day as a Journeyman

It is years later. I have eliminated most of the night calls and I am selling at least one policy a day. Some of these policies do necessitate an occasional evening appointment.

I am selling all types of life insurance now, and not restricting myself to retirement income forms. I know a great deal more about my merchandise. The "facts of life" about high-level free energy salesmanship are beginning to dawn on me. A small private office has been assigned to me by my General Agent, "Coop" Curry. I usually go directly there and do some prospecting on the commute train en route to the office.

This particular morning I drive. A traffic officer orders me to the side of the road. Before he can even ask to see my license, I start talking life insurance to him. The moment he hears this, to escape me, he speeds away without giving me a ticket.

My immediate prospect lists are still derived chiefly from the newspaper, but now I have a secretary who clips them out for me. Also, I am developing referred leads.

I use direct-mail advertising pieces with business reply

cards to send to the names taken from the newspapers. This is also handled by my secretary.

Some of the "names" have returned these reply cards. I will call some of them, but first I shall go through the WHO—WHY—WHAT—WHERE—WHEN—WOW—HOW process. Also, if I can, I will find someone who knows them.

I call first the people processed through the "seven W's."

It is always a surprise to the prospect (or his wife if she answers the phone) that I already know something about him.

I set up definite appointments by my WHERE and WHEN.

I try to arrange for a lunch interview.

There is still some free time. I take some "names" from the list of prospects who failed to reply to my direct mail, and mentally put each one through the "seven W's." Some of them stand out. I phone them, using the following type of approach:

"Good morning. This is Karl Bach of the Penn Mutual Life Insurance Company. I am making a personal survey. How long has it been since a life insurance agent has called on you? Are there any questions about the latest new developments in life insurance that you would like to have answered?"

This is sufficient to get me several evening appointments.

I have had lunch with a fine prospect, a promising one. The restaurant is located in one of the suburbs and since I have no other appointments at the office, I call on a few old clients and new prospects in that area. My final call of the day is to deliver a new policy. Then home to my family.

All of this may sound like a page out of any salesman's diary, but the point in relating a typical day during my journeyman stage is to demonstrate that it is not too unlike a day in the preceding apprentice stage.

The basic theme is the same—to fulfill the needs for life insurance.

The variations are minor—they relate chiefly to changes in my family, my higher standard of living, and the growth in my office organization so that my time and energy is freed for selling.

Another difference from the apprentice stage is that I have upgraded my prospecting and can now make most of my calls during the day, a welcome development.

In the Course of One Day as an Advanced Salesman

My office has expanded. I now have a staff of four employees plus a junior associate. This means a payroll and overhead.

Many of my appointments are with business executives who prefer to see me in the morning before they become involved with their day's work. I see them en route to my office.

Fewer names are clipped from the newspapers. My clients now number several thousand. They keep me busy. The attendant detail work keeps my employees busy, sometimes overtime. Almost all of my new prospects are referrals from old clients. Some I turn over to my associate.

Last night I selected from the prospect and client file the names of men who should be phoned today.

I have several trunk lines and a number of telephones. My office staff screen the incoming calls. Only the absolute "must" incoming calls get through to me until I have made my date with a prospect for lunch.

The lunch date is always important; sometimes it is prolonged. This afternoon will be devoted to comprehensive estate planning for an important client.

At 6:00 I am on my way home.

Tonight is unusual. I make a call on the way home. I have made no earlier sale today, but on that last call, I will make my sale. It is only a $5,000 policy, but I have kept my commitment to myself.

No matter how many or how large the sales I made yesterday, *I will make at least one sale today*.

The theme of the advanced or professional stage has not changed from the first two stages.

The most notable difference is simply a matter of degree: more clients, more employees, more office equipment, etc. In general, it is just a larger operation.

My job is still that of bringing financial and economic security to people, and to me this is synonymous with the introduction of ever more life insurance into their affairs.

As an advanced salesman, I have kept pace with the growth and development of my clients. If I have expanded, it is only because they have expanded. As they grew, so did I.

24

Beyond the Journeyman Stage

There Are No Maestros

In the sense in which I use the term "advanced salesmen," I mean they are merely more developed journeymen.

Even after I reached the advanced platcau, I still felt I needed all the learning I could get.

As a famous philosopher once said: "There is no knowledge, only varying degrees of ignorance."

A Big Article Needs a Big Container—Attitude Beats Aptitude, at Any Stage

To sell a $100,000 life insurance policy which rounds out a client's estate to a million dollars, you must think in terms of a million. Yet, there is more to it than a series of zeros.

The big client has greater buying potential, but he must be sold from his point of view. He is big because he thinks big, and this is contagious. It makes you expand your own vistas.

In the life insurance industry, we have a "Million-Dollar Round Table"—a prestige organization of men who sell a million dollars or more of life insurance each year. I understand there are similar organizations in other areas of business.

Why not have a five-million-dollar club? Are there so few salesmen who strive to reach that figure?

A topflight journeyman can make the Million-Dollar Round Table. What I am talking about in advanced free energy salesmanship is how to get on up beyond that figure.

At the Million-Dollar Round Table meetings, the chief topic is how to sell the big prospect, the large buyer. The little man is to be sold on a catch-as-catch-can basis. I do not agree with that attitude. My service is not only for the very affluent, the well-to-do, but also for the great number of "little leaguers."

When working with a man of average means, I do not limit myself to that one sale. I plan out a full program for his family as a unit, and then help him put it into effect. Even as in the case of the large buyer, if necessary I call in the family financial expert, the prospect's lawyer and accountant, and do a comprehensive job.

One of the great challenges and personal satisfactions I realize in the life insurance business is meeting the varying needs of such a wide variety of prospects. They run the full gamut—large and small, and I want to help work out their individual problems in practical, economical terms. Only then can the insurance salesman affirm that he has given meaning to his selling career.

I have found that once you get "up there" among the advanced men, there is a lot more to be gained by soliciting the little fellow than in doing all of your dreaming about the big one.

Also, the little fellow you service today may well be the big one who comes back to you tomorrow. The baby of today is the man of the future.

Learn How to Delegate Work

My secretaries are licensed insurance agents in their own right, or else are preparing for their license.

Thus they have learned the problems related to insurance selling. They know what I am doing, what I am facing, and how to help me.

I never wait for my secretaries to ask me for a raise. I beat them to the punch, give them raises and bonuses before they feel they deserve them. I don't demand strict hours of working time. I do everything I can to acknowledge their value to me.

My Office Is My Best Sales Tool

When the apprentice gets well along the road to the journeyman stage, he will begin to energize prospects and clients who will come to his office. Here he has his tools at hand. In the advanced stage, the salesman's office should be his second home.

An office *can* be used as a place where the salesman has a psychological advantage in the interview and the prospect is likewise at an advantage, because of freedom from interruptions.

In free energy salesmanship, a "sales tool" is any device to stimulate and help the prospect buy. In my office such tools are assembled in one place.

I Borrowed the Idea

Every salesman needs refueling. Refueling means listening to other salesmen and observing their methods.

I was well up in the ranks of advanced salesmen in my business, but I wanted to make more progress and I couldn't quite figure out how to accomplish it.

At a convention, Gerry Weber, a truly advanced salesman, related how he developed his telephone and "see me at my office" technique. He mastered this to such a degree, he no longer had to leave his office for business calls.

All around me I could hear men whispering, "bunk!" But my mind is always open. I like to adopt the ideas of others. I listened carefully to every word he said, just as I would do in an interview. I noted every inflection in his voice. His inflections conveyed what mere words could not say.

When I returned home, I began to figure out how I could use his "office salesmanship" method. I studied and adjusted his technique to suit my temperament and personality.

Thereafter, my office became my best sales tool.

First Impressions—Office Appearance

What is the first impression on a client or prospect coming into your office? Project yourself and think, objectively, about what you see; it is of primary importance.

I did not design or decorate my own office. Experts did it for me. I never do for myself what others can do better.

The prospect enters. He sees my secretary-associates, and possibly some of my other associates. I do not have an elaborate reception room. Since I don't keep people waiting, I do not require it.

The door to my private office is only a few feet beyond the entrance. A low wall separates the prospect from my secretaries. He cannot overhear their conversations or read the material upon which they are working. He cannot help but observe, therefore, that the records and affairs of my clients are kept strictly confidential.

Ordinarily, I come out of my office to greet the prospect, rather than have him ushered in to see me. He is my guest throughout the interview.

It is often said that San Francisco is "naturally air-conditioned." But I insist on having the temperature in my private office scientifically controlled. I do not wish to take a chance on the possibility that my prospect, especially during an intensive interview, will be uncomfortable.

Even a cursory glance indicates that the tools for business are all there. A large commodious executive desk, with evidence of work on it, but uncluttered; comfortable chairs; a small sofa for more relaxed comfort; a compact but highly organized business library; telephones, intercom equipment, calculating machine, writing materials and facilities, and drinking water.

One or two sales-contest trophies and a certificate of "Award for Achievement" are also there. I could cover the walls with them, but *my prospect's interests* are the topic I want to discuss.

Two of the walls are almost entirely windowed, but they are shielded by full-length, subtly colored drapes. The lighting is indirect and the ceiling is soundproofed. No sounds from the outer office can penetrate.

There is no clock to watch.

Phone calls rarely interrupt the interview. If an important call does come in, my secretary brings me a note to that effect. I will not interrupt the interview to take that call unless it is absolutely unavoidable. And if I should, I never let one client overhear the business discussion of another. That room and all that goes on in it says, "Let's get at your affairs, with your best interests in mind, right now. This is *your* time and you deserve all of it."

Talk Business Before or After Lunch

My office is across the street from four of San Francisco's best restaurants, and in the immediate vicinity of many other fine ones. I take a client or prospect to luncheon nearly every day.

There are two periods in which to talk business: one is just before lunch, while the client or prospect is hungry; the other is immediately after lunch, when he feels contented.

I often hold lunch in abeyance until the sale is made. I handle it by saying, "Let's get our business completed first. By that time, we won't have to wait in line for a table."

Hunger accelerates action. Action is the reason I want him in my office before lunch. Occasionally, I wait until after lunch to talk business in my office in order to avoid discussing his affairs in a noisy, crowded restaurant.

I also provide free parking space for my clients or prospects to facilitate their visits to my office and eliminate parking-meter worries.

To induce him to come to my office, I use a power expression, such as "When would you like to come over?"

I *don't* say, "Will you come to my office?"

In wording your questions to a prospect, never invite a possible "no" answer.

News Items and How to Use Them

Previously I pointed out the importance of news items as a source.

When I read on the business page of the newspaper or hear about the promotion of a really "big name," I know immediately that this will necessitate changes in that man's insurance program.

Other insurance salesman recognize this too. Most of them will promptly send him congratulatory letters. Investment and other types of salesmen will pursue him hotly.

I don't subscribe to this type of approach. Rather, I begin my campaign by sending him a copy of the tax bulletin we issue especially for "advanced" prospects. After about six weeks, when the furor has subsided, I telephone him and ask about his reaction to our brochures. I tell him about certain changes in the tax laws—to stimulate his desire to meet with me. Thus, I make a potential prospect out of him.

It doesn't always work, of course. But it has been my experience that this approach produces many more sales than were I to pounce on him a moment after his advancement and try to push my way into his office.

I find that with situations like this, I realize greater returns when the prospect thinks he initiates the idea for an appointment.

You Can Hit a Target at Any Range

Through the casualty insurance division of my business, I am able to provide my clients with a rounded insurance program.

With any type of policy a client buys, I make him promise that wherever he may be, if he has any insurance questions or problems, he will call me *collect*. This is an old established practice of mine.

This is a long-range plan. I want to be known as *the man whose advice is constantly available to his clients.*

A young physician bought an automobile insurance policy from me. Shortly after, he moved several hundred miles away from San Francisco. Years later, I received a phone call collect from him.

"Karl, a fellow smashed my car door. What shall I do?"

I advised him. We chatted a minute or so. Then he said, "By the way, I have a good practice here. What would a deposit of $200 a month provide for my retirement?"

That collect call paid off. The collect call is an excellent sales device.

Another young man purchased a modest life insurance policy from me. Soon after, he became a naval officer. From time to time I received collect calls from him and his wife originating from many points throughout the United States. They had questions about how to adjust and coordinate their insurance to the retirement and pension plans made available to servicemen by the government.

One day I received a collect call from Norfolk, Virginia.

"Hello Karl. You have been so nice about collect calls, we thought we would just chat with you a few minutes."

"I'm delighted to hear from you," I said.

We talked and then his wife came to the phone. "Incidentally, Karl, my husband just got a big promotion. We want a $100,000 policy and $10,000 each on me and the children."

They were all in the East. I arranged for their physical examinations with doctors in their areas, and handled all the other details very adequately by correspondence.

Out of a clear blue sky one morning I picked up the receiver to hear: "Hello, Karl. Seven years ago when I worked in my husband's office you gave me a ball-point pen. I promised that one day I would call you. Well, this is the day."

That call turned out to mean the sale of a $250,000 life insurance policy.

Watch the Acorns Grow into Giant Oaks

I have a number of clients who started very modestly, but whose personal insurance holdings today are well in excess of $1 million each.

I build a client up one step at a time, layer by layer, and every new sale to him is made because the previous one was based on his best interests. The client's best interests are the real test of free energy salesmanship.

Clients are built by sound advice. Reputation for good guidance attracts the highest type of prospect. The advanced salesman is interested chiefly in repeat business. He has little use for the one-shot deal.

25

You Need Never
Be Otiose

I have been told that every book should introduce at least one term that is not in common use. I have reserved that for this discussion where it is innocuous and will be out of the way.

My term is *otiose*. It means "idle, indolent, ineffective, futile, superfluous, or useless."

Our system of economy has been trying, through the common practice of mandatory retirement, to make all employed men otiose at age 65. The men who are thus forced to retire to otiosity (and oblivion) do this involuntarily in a great number of cases.

The free energy salesman is not subject to any mandatory retirement restrictions. As long as a man is able to sell, even if only by means of a telephone, the opportunity for free energy salesmanship is available to him.

As a free energy salesman you will never be victimized, as in numerous other occupations, after a lifetime of dedicated work in selling.

Free energy salesmanship is certainly one of the most stimulating and rewarding lives in the world. And no man can
force you to get out of it.

It is my hope that some of us who are successful free
energy salesmen can also find a way to keep our less fortunate fellow salesmen out of enforced otiosity. At least it's
worth a try.

Now, there are even "hidden profits" for the self-employed
life insurance salesman. As a result of longer life spans, he
can continue to receive renewal commissions over a longer
period than ever before.

PART IV
Estate Planning

Helping People to Die
"For All They Are Worth"
Taxwise

26

Is It the Fourth Stage?

A trend is developing in the life insurance business, which, in my opinion, is unfortunate.

I am referring to the notion that in life insurance selling, estate planning is a thing apart; that it represents the professional stage—one step above that of the advanced salesman.

My fervent belief that family financial planning supersedes all other types of economic planning has been emphasized throughout this book.

To me, the service of estate planning for clients is not a special art, or a new departure. It is merely a new name for an old process in life insurance selling, which from the very first stage, must dedicate itself to helping men keep financially fit to live and die.

Estate planning is like the trunk of the tree, which supports the branches represented by the apprentice, journeyman, and advanced periods in the development process of the life insurance salesman.

No life insurance salesman should permit himself to believe that, regardless of his measure of success, he can get completely beyond the working-at-a-trade stage.

He must always keep in mind that estate planning is only an extension of his dominant objective, which is to afford the clients and their families the infinite benefits inherent in a well-planned life insurance program.

When a life insurance salesman arrogantly asserts that he is "practicing a profession"—that he is an estate planner, I am not particularly impressed. What it does mean to me is that he has refined his methods, developed his "old stand-by" techniques, picked up some pointers and new skills he missed on the way up. The sand-lot ballplayer and the major leaguer use the same basic equipment, and play the game by the same rules.

The insurance salesman must recognize the fact that he is not a bearer or creator of fortunes. At the apprentice stage he is merely a midwife in attendance at the "delivery" of life insurance funds to the client and his family.

When he emerges onto the estate planning or "professional" plateau, he is more comparable to the experienced obstetrician. He has retained his original skills, and is still working at his old trade of delivery money to keep families in financial safety-zones. The crude elementary methods of the apprentice have been replaced by the new techniques and concepts of the advanced salesman.

Do you remember this one? The patient had a rash on the back of his hands which the doctor studied thoughtfully. He searched his medical experience for some clue as to the nature of the patient's condition, but with little success. Finally, the doctor gazed out of the window and asked, "Have you had this before?"

"Yes," replied the patient.

"Well," said the doctor, in his most solemn, professional voice, "you've got it again."

Everything that the estate planner is doing currently, at what he considers the professional stage, he was doing throughout his evolution from apprentice to advanced salesman. He was just adapting the traditional to a modern pattern of activity.

The limitless scope of estate planning, or my conception of "family financial planning," is too comprehensive a subject to be condensed here. If I survive the reaction to this book, there will be another, which will survey and appraise the broad area of "fringe benefits," pensions, and profit-sharing plans. Also, the "siblings" of life insurance, health and accident protection, are a separate subject and deserve independent treatment.

Here, I shall confine myself to how I energize prospects into a financial-health examination, leading to family financial planning.

I look back with amusement on the many instances in which this simple but profound quatrain opened wide the minds of resistant prospects:

> *Five duties line each mortal path*
> *That leads to life's far border;*
> *To live, to learn, to serve, to earn,*
> *To set one's house in order.*

Or, another approach which I used when calling on an opinionated widow whose husband's liberal will left her rich. It is less poetic, but meaningful.

I said, "Don't you want to leave your children as well off as your husband left you?"

This was enough to stimulate a successful interview. The results were gratifying indeed.

As an estate planner, I consider myself a charter member of the "Society for the Care and Preservation of Families," especially growing ones.

For me, the most effective estate plan is the one that produces the best results for a client's family, the greatest economic unit of all.

If I can help my clients live with a purpose and die in "style," through the proper organization of their affairs with life insurance, then I am performing my job in the full sense.

In my service of family financial planning, I feel that I am practicing as a "Doctor of Family Financial Economics," title or not. If through my counsel and service in estate planning I can contribute to family financial security, which in turn contributes to family solidarity, I am rewarded beyond measure.

Yes, I am fascinated by the business of life insurance selling, and the part that I play in it daily, in robbing death of its complete victory, by supplying funds to the boys, girls, wives, and others that men leave behind.

Some of the ideas in this chapter have cut a lot of life insurance timber for me, fashioned into sales, because I have prevented prospects from being indifferent about providing for their futures—the futures of their families and themselves. And I rejoice in the knowledge that I have helped many men "look after" their widows through life insurance, thereby preserving their self-respect and sparing them the indignity of living *with* or *on* their children.

Prestige Labels: Profession, Vocation, Calling, or Simply a Dignified Job?

I am firmly convinced that you cannot "decentralize" estate planning. Even at the apprentice stage, the life insurance salesman who has a thorough understanding of fundamentals is already qualified to advise.

The solution of your client's financial and family security problems need not wait until you have reached the professional stage. At any stage of his evolution, a life insurance salesman can practice the high standards of those allegedly "professional" in the ministry of life insurance selling.

In short, there is no arbitrary time for the professional approach.

For a number of years, I have been active in estate planning work, but at no time have I felt that I was working in some special category. I have been occupied with selling and servicing my clients, exactly as I did during the earlier stages.

The major difference was the emphasis on teamwork. Formerly I left the technical aspects of estate planning to the experts, and limited the scope of my operations to the sale of life insurance, doing this job exclusively, soundly, and properly.

Every life insurance man should be a "general practitioner" and not a "specialist."

The function of a life insurance salesman is exactly the same at any stage in his development.

The overemphasis of the "professional" approach in the sale of life insurance is a highly distorted view. It is a false prestige label exploited by men who are more concerned with inflating their egos than the welfare of their clients.

This is my uncompromising attitude. As I've stressed before, the main function of a life insurance salesman is to help men "keep financially fit to live and die." If the salesman fails to promote measures to protect the security of a client and the welfare of his family, of what value is his self-designated status as that of having a "profession"?

In the final analysis, it is precisely how a salesman performs in the interests of his client that matters, and certainly not the title or rank or any other superficial designation attached to him.

I Sell Merchandise

Some look upon salesmanship as a "profession," and therefore hold that the salesman should render professional service. This may be true, but only if you can give valued advice to a client.

When you are rendering a service, uninfluenced by the sale of merchandise, then you are judicious, unbiased, and "professional." Otherwise, you are merely working at a trade, in which the profit motive is selfishly predominant.

Most of the time I sell merchandise. I give the customer a tangible product which is worth enough to him to pay money for it. Tangible products that sell for money are merchandise. The selling of them is a trade.

My professional advice is included as a bonus with every policy I sell; however, that isn't what the client primarily pays for.

These are my green trading stamps. The customer pays only for the merchandise he buys.

In my work, the professional advice is not restricted to the sale. It is available to my clients throughout the life span of my merchandise.

When I deliver a policy, I don't tell the customer that "the results of my professional services are ready for delivery." I phone him and say, "The merchandise is ready. When can we get together?"

The life insurance a prospect can buy—the type and rate— depend on how well he qualifies in a physical examination. I don't tell him, "we must know how good a risk you are before we can give you our professional services." I am more likely to say, "until I learn how you qualify, I won't be able to determine what merchandise will be available to you."

The Education of a Life Insurance Salesman, and of Salesmen Generally

Every life insurance salesman is like an island surrounded by an ocean of company training courses, from the elementary to the most advanced.

In addition, there are countless "services," gushing a flood of ink in the form of every variety of book and brochure, designed for the continuing enlightenment and training of life insurance salesmen.

This is, of course, as it should be. The life insurance salesman, in expanding his area of operations, must have an inquiring mind.

In my opinion, however, many of these courses and services are extremely limited. Instead of stimulating the individual to creative thinking or imaginative resourcefulness, they tend to make all salesmen conform to the same pattern. It's as if they were all products of the same mold.

High standards of performance from insurance salesmen demand character more than polish. True education is not confined to the knowledge of techniques or the accumulation of facts; rather, it is concerned with gaining a realistic concept of selling and the most effective application of sales ideas. Also, it should teach him to think like an insurance salesman.

All of this may not be according to the proverbial Hoyle. I hope that in your appraisal of these opinions, you will be diplomatic. This has been defined as the art of disagreeing, without being disagreeable.

Indeed, much of what has been said above may seem rebellious or unorthodox. I am not trying to be hypercritical of existing methods of training salesmen. Nor am I trying to make a radical departure from recognized systems, standard procedures, or accepted forms. Whether in education or in the field of selling ideas, I advocate adherence to traditional concepts and retention of time-tested methods, but these should be constantly subject to review and re-evaluation, and then be adjusted accordingly.

Keep old skills, but extend their use. Keep old recipes, but try out new ones. Satisfaction with things as they are is not a sign of progress.

I believe that in many cases, it is the prospect or the client who is in need of more orientation. Unfortunately, more training for the salesman will not serve to educate the client.

Clients and prospects have to be taught that life insurance is thoughtfulness.

Wives, the notorious obstructionists to the purchase of more life insurance by their husbands, must be educated to the fact that this does not represent unselfishness. Actually, by offering this resistance to the purchase of more life insurance, these wives are *not* sparing their husbands the strain of premium payments.

Life insurance salesmen must "teach" wives that unless they encourage husbands to purchase more and more life insurance, these wives may one day shortchange themselves of the full measure of financial security which might have been theirs.

Psychologists notwithstanding, it takes money, among other things of course, to realize emotional security.

27

A Letter to My
Fellow Salesmen

Clearing the Slate

This book is not intended to be an autobiography. That would seem highly presumptuous to me. The mantle of self-importance is an ill-fitting garment.

Nor was this intended as a slick success-story, but rather an expression of my philosophy of life insurance selling developed through wide experience.

The material I've used is a record of some of my everyday selling activity. The cases described herein are real cases. They worked for me, but don't get the impression that by using a pat phrase or slogan I made the sale. In fact, reliance on such devices may often defeat a sale.

I feel that in showing you how I work at my trade, it might demonstrate the straight, simple basis for successful salesmanship. There is no magic or mystery. There are no secrets.

Throughout my insurance selling career I have been eating peaches from trees that were planted by someone else. Now,

I feel the time has arrived when I should plant some trees to reciprocate for the fruit I've enjoyed.

I want to reinvest my profits in the industry that nurtured me. My fundamental purpose here is to share my thinking and experiences with other salesmen, whether they are "old pros" who have been through the mill, or neophytes just embarking on their apprenticeship stage. Although I am an adopted son, I have come to believe in the American tradition of togetherness with my fellow practitioners.

I am seeking neither admiration nor disciples, because I consider life insurance selling a highly personalized type of selling. Consequently, such selling doesn't lend itself readily to glib generalizations.

If you are looking for some short cut to acquiring a quick fortune, I've demonstrated clearly that you cannot hope to do this selling life insurance. However, a salesman who fails to prosper at life insurance selling is simply one who has not served an adequate apprenticeship. As in the case of a golfer, there is either a breakdown in his swing (approach), or in his follow-through (close).

The components of my own successful efforts were hardly words alone. I cannot agree with judges who have insisted that "cases that are not well argued are not well decided." I favor provocative ideas, not controversies, with my clients.

The basic principles which helped me were the generous use of creative imagination coupled with dynamism and enterprise—the combined efforts of footwork and headwork. Creative imagination, of course, is essential to the growth of any business.

The life insurance industry is rooted in science, actuarial and statistical, but its business has flourished in psychology, in understanding human nature.

The human touch is all-important. I advanced financially

as I broadened my understanding of human nature—not because I developed more techniques and showmanship.

It was "vertical meditation"—thinking on my feet, combined with strong drives and nervous free energy—but not the neurotic kind that breeds ulcers and anxieties.

I got tired of being poor. When I recognized that life insurance selling was a business of ideas, rather than an exercise in ingenuity, then I knew that I couldn't fail.

Naturally, the climb upward is fraught with frustrations and obstacles. There are hardships at every stage of every salesman's development. As his business grows, it becomes a more complex operation. However, I have found that making the sale is the great panacea for a salesman's problems, and the most potent remedy for growing pains in a selling career.

The key word is persistence. If you prefer the same concept expressed in rhyme, here it is:

No one needs as much endurance
As the man who sells life insurance.

PART V
A Panoramic Survey

28

A Panoramic Survey

I have learned some significant lessons in selling on my way up through the various levels of development. By putting them into practice, I have been able to establish a comfortable cushion of financial security for myself, while also providing financial shock-absorbers for my clients and their families. Any life insurance man can do this. Indeed, any life insurance salesman might have sold the same clients, except that I, through my experience, learned these 16 key lessons:

(1) When to *stop* selling and pause sufficiently to let the prospect give me the order.

(2) To use basic selling methods in cutting down lost motion.

(3) Not to *know* when a prospect meant *no.*

(4) That the overworked excuse of the prospects—"I have no money," or "I can't afford it"—evaporated when I demonstrated how simple it was to transfer some of their present capital into life insurance. Here the working power of this money, in the best interests of their families and themselves, would be greatly multiplied.

(5) That you must not expect prospects to understand you unless you first understand them.

(6) To turn unproductive social time into very profitable action time by sharing mealtime with prospects and clients.

(7) To constantly re-evaluate my work methods and adapt myself to changing trends, and to *change direction* when dictated by circumstances.

(8) That in order to elicit from other people their "best," you must give yours. Innate sincerity will gain the prospect's good will.

(9) That my first sale to a client is the beginning of a long and meaningful association that can endure a lifetime, if I continue to work in his behalf.

(10) That if you are to succeed as a financial advisor to others, you must practice the principles you advocate.

(11) That to provide the best possible service to your clients, it was important to enlist the aid, skill, and talents of others. The do-it-yourself folly can be prohibitive in cost.

(12) That you must limit yourself to reasonable and attainable goals, but that failure indicates only that you are not living up to your full capabilities.

(13) That creative life insurance selling requires creative imagination and resourcefulness—not dexterity with figures.

(14) That the *apprentice, journeyman* and *advanced* stages are not separate entities; moreover, there is no fixed period when you emerge from one to the other. Each level of development overlaps with the other and many aspects of the beginning stage are carried forward and incorporated into the most advanced.

(15) That regardless of techniques, there is no real substitute for constantly bringing the salesman's message of life insurance to the American people.

(16) That in doing so, I must keep my sales story true and

simple. Prospects understand my direct appeal to them to provide future financial security for their families and themselves.

These are the lessons I learned as I worked through the various stages of life insurance salesmanship. They have taken me a long way up the road. You can learn them, and they will lead you there, providing you resolve, deep within yourself, to get there.

I earnestly hope that these lessons, the partners in my success, may be even more productive for you than they have been for me.

The attributes and attitudes that were so vital to my own growth, you also possess, or you can develop and acquire them. No one salesman has a monopoly on selling talents. There are no born supersalesmen. There are only salesmen who are *supersensitive* to the needs of their clients.

Every salesman must expect some incidence of frustration and disappointment, but he must always land solidly on both feet.

Setbacks are an integral part of the picture of growth, but never let them interfere with your courage and appetite for further ventures. The reduction in number of prospects who didn't buy will bring you closer to the ones who will buy, if you subscribe to the time-tested and proven idea that a certain number of calls will inevitably result in a certain percentage of sales.

The adoption of new ideas and applying them to the sale of life insurance has become a philosophy to live with, for me.

I am filled with confidence for the future, and in my personal ability to contribute and share in the promise of that future. I have the same confidence, that you have the same abilities and that you will contribute and share in that future, in possibly greater measure.

May we meet soon along the road to greater financial security and stability for our growing nation, through the ever increasing use of life insurance. This will help maintain the high American standard of living. Thus, all of us, including the life insurance salesmen, will gain.

Make your future in life insurance selling a great challenge and adventure. By means of a thorough understanding of the fundamentals, and realizing that selling life insurance is not an exercise in ingenuity, as it may sometimes seem, you, too, will make your fortune in life insurance selling through the application of free energy salesmanship.

You can do it better! Your success is assured if you are *sold* on whatever product you sell.